JESUS APPEALS TO THE WORLD

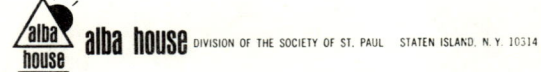

JESUS APPEALS TO THE WORLD

THE UNCEASING ACT OF LOVE REVEALED TO
THE CAPUCHIN NUN, SISTER MARY CONSOLATA
(1903 - 1946)

By

LORENZO SALES, I.M.C.

Translated by Alfred J. M. Mausolff

IMPRIMI POTEST
Staten Island, Feb. 1, 1955

VICTOR VIBERTI, S.S.P.
Censor Del.

NIHIL OBSTAT

JOHN M. FEARNS, S.T.D.
Censor Librorum

IMPRIMATUR
New York, March 11, 1955

✠ FRANCIS CARDINAL SPELLMAN,
Archbishop of New York

SIXTH EDITION, 1971

All rights reserved, including the right to reproduce this book, or portions thereof, in any form, except for brief quotations in a review.

COPYRIGHT, 1955, BY SOCIETY OF ST. PAUL., CANFIELD, OHIO
PRINTED IN U. S. A., BY SOCIETY OF ST. PAUL., NEW YORK, N. Y.

DECLARATION

The author declares that the contents of this book are based on purely human convictions and that the expressions "divine instructions," "sayings of Jesus and of Mary," "revelations," "visions," etc. are in no way intended to anticipate the judgment of Mother Church whose obedient and loving son the author declares himself to be.

Index

	Page
Preface to the English Translation	9
Introduction	11

I. SPIRITUAL CHILDHOOD AND THE LIFE OF LOVE

In the footprints of the Little Flower	15
The selfsame spirit	18
What Jesus prefers	23
What pleases Jesus	26

II. THE LIFE OF LOVE AND CHRISTIAN VIRTUES

Have faith in love	31
Hope in love	37
Trust in love	47
Be in love with Love	64

III. THE LIFE OF LOVE AND CHRISTIAN PERFECTION

Love is sanctity	71
Intimate life of love with Jesus	76
Fervor of love in purity of spirit	80
The loving soul gives all to Jesus	95
Love receives all from Jesus	100
Fruits of the life of love	106

IV. LIVING AN ACT OF PERFECT LOVE

The convenience of a formula	114
The formula for the unceasing act of love	115
How the unceasing act of love is to be understood	117
The divine requests for the unceasing act of love	120
The spiritual fruitfulness of the unceasing act of love	127

V. PERFECTING THE LIFE OF LOVE THROUGH PERFECTING THE UNCEASING ACT OF LOVE

Premise	133
Continuity of love in the unceasing act of love	135

JESUS APPEALS TO THE WORLD

	Page
Purity of love in the act of love	143
Intensity of love in the act of love	149
Love of abandonment and the unceasing act of love	152

VI. THE UNCEASING ACT OF LOVE IN THE SPIRITUAL LIFE OF SISTER CONSOLATA

The act of love and vocal prayer	161
The act of love and meditation	165
The act of love and spiritual reading	168
The act of love and the particular examen	173
The act of love and the spiritual retreat	174
The act of love in various spiritual states	176
The height of heroism in the unceasing act of love	180

VII. A TANGIBLE FRUIT OF THE DIVINE MESSAGE: THE WORK OF THE LITTLEST ONES

Jesus reveals to Sister Consolata the work of the Littlest Ones	183
The consecration of the First Littlest One	187
Sister Consolata and the work of the Littlest Ones	190
The Littlest Ones and Our Lady	192
The Littlest Ones and Sister Consolata	194
The death of the first Littlest One	195
Sister Consolata's message to the Littlest Ones	200
To all who are not Littlest Ones	204
The unceasing act of love and the practice of virtue	206

VIII. SUMMARY

Back to the Source	209
The law of love	211
The evil and its remedy	212
The new gift of the Heart of Jesus	215
To Thee, O Lord!	217

IX. APPENDIX

Some clarifications regarding the work of the Littlest Ones	219
Prayer for obtaining graces through the intercession of Sister Consolata	224

Preface To The English Translation

THE Italian original of Father Sales' important little book has already seen four editions; its French translation two, and the German version, five! And at this writing, Christ's inspiring new Message is also appearing in Dutch, Croatian, Spanish and Portuguese.

The book has also been translated into Serbian, Bulgarian, Czech, Rumanian, Polish, Slovakian, Slovene, Russian, Japanese, Chinese and Greek, but these manuscripts have not been published because of the prevailing political conditions.

Through this present translation, the English speaking world will now become acquainted with Our Lord's latest, most tender appeal for love:

"I prefer an act of love and a Communion of love to any other gift."

"I thirst for love!"

"If people would only love Me, what felicity would reign in this unhappy world!"

"Love Me, and you will be happy; the more you love Me, the happier you will be!"

"Do not lose time! Every act of love means a soul!"

"By means of unceasing prayer, prepare the triumph of My Heart and of My love throughout the earth!"

A. J. M. M.

Introduction

SISTER MARY CONSOLATA, in the world Pierina Betrone, was born on April 6th, 1903 at Saluzzo, Piedmont, and in the following year her family moved to Turin. While she was making her thanksgiving after Communion on the feast of the Immaculate Conception in 1916—she was then 13 years old—she heard for the first time an inner Voice which asked, "Do you wish to be entirely Mine?" Without comprehending the full implications of the question, she replied, "Yes, Jesus!" To belong entirely to Jesus meant for her to become a nun. She strove hard for her vocation and for a time was even subjected to a painful spiritual trial, but finally, on April 17th, 1929, the Solemnity of Saint Joseph, she was able to realize her ardent aspirations and was received into the Capuchin convent of Turin.

Ten years later Sister Consolata passed over to the new convent at Moriondo (Testona), which had been founded to take care of the greatly increased community, and there she crowned her short but intense life with a holy death on July 18th, 1946, at the age of 43. Her earthly remains are interred in the cemetery of Moncalieri.

Although Sister Consolata was favored by God with great spiritual gifts, these nevertheless passed unobserved in her small community; nor did they ever cause her to relax her earnest striving for the summit of sanctity. Every step on the way to perfection cost her self-denial, and to the very end of her life she had to struggle valiantly against her own shortcomings; nor were all manner of violent temptations spared her; but she was outstanding for generosity, tenacity, and zeal as a combatant, and her dedication to God and neighbor knew no bounds.

Sister Consolata was given a particular mission and vocation by God like that of Saint Teresa of the Child Jesus, whose glorious disciple she was. Her mission, for the fulfillment of which she offered herself as a victim-soul in response to a divine request, was for the benefit of all those men and women whom she liked to call her Brothers and Sisters—the souls of priests and Religious who had gone astray; and most consoling are the promises which Jesus made to her in this regard.

Sister Consolata's particular vocation was one of love, to round out, so to speak, the Little Flower's doctrine of the Little Way of Love by giving it a concrete form which could be practiced and achieved by all souls who feel themselves called to it. This doctrine or way of love may be summed up in the following three points which are the nucleus of Our Lord's instructions to Sister Consolata:

1. To offer an unceasing act of love from the heart,
2. To have a smiling "yes" for everyone, to see and treat Jesus in everyone,
3. To have a grateful "yes" for everything (for every divine request).

These three points are also frequently expressed in this formula: "Never omit one act of love, one act of charity, or one sacrifice from one Communion to the next."

Here then is a veritable program of spiritual training which takes in the duties of the soul toward God, her neighbor, and herself. And it must be noted that, according to Our Lord's own assurances, it is the faithfulness with which the soul maintains the unceasing act of love that makes it easy for her to be always ready with a "yes" for everyone and everything. This unceasing act of love, therefore, constitutes the essential purpose of this new and merciful manifestation of the Sacred Heart of Jesus, and so this book will concern itself exclusively with the unceasing act of love. Our own part in this work has consisted merely in compiling and arranging the material in a logical sequence; we have added only what seemed necessary in order to tie the various parts together and to offer certain short explanations and reflections.

Sister Consolata's style was plain and unaffected. We would not know how to improve upon it; and even if we could, we would not dare to cross God's designs, for it is our conviction that Jesus chose, for the purpose of revealing this doctrine, the least adapted instrument, so that it would be all the more apparent that it was He who was doing and is still doing everything. In this way also it would not be possible for man's frequently confused interpretations to distort His simple and clear doctrine, each word of which is light, truth, and life.

Ought one to consider that this book, or rather the doctrine it contains, is intended for everyone? In our opinion one must distinguish between a life of love in general and the practice of the life of love according to a definite method. Under the first aspect these pages are beyond doubt meant for everyone, for the great commandment to love God applies to all; the divine instructions contained in this book are in substance nothing but an insistent appeal to observe that commandment, and that concerns not only love but the perfection of love.

The case is different, however, in regard to the practice of the life of love in accordance with the method which Jesus taught to Sister Consolata. These divine lessons, though most useful to everyone under certain aspects, are quite evidently addressed to a rather limited number of souls, that is to those religious or laypeople who are favored with a particular vocation to love, and therefore with an attraction to the life of love, and who wish to live it in all its perfection.

In any case, one thing appears certain: nothing contained in this book can in any way interfere with the spirit which is the peculiar feature of every religious congregation, whether contemplative or active. On the contrary, it is likely to prove a great aid in maintaining it in vigor and making it reflourish by leading souls to the perfect exercise of the love of God, of neighborly charity, and of Christian mortification, which are the three essential requisites of the religious life and of perfection; and all this is in addition to the divine promises which we will relate. Jesus desires the spiritual renovation of the world, and He desires it to come about through a more vigorous renewal of the supernatural life in souls, and particularly in those souls who are consecrated to Him. These are to form the divine leaven which will cause the mass to ferment.

Through the Immaculate Heart of Mary we entrust this modest work to the Sacred Heart of Jesus, and ask a blessing upon it, that Christ's reign of love may spread throughout the world.

Fr. Lorenzo Sales, I.M.C.

- I -

SPIRITUAL CHILDHOOD AND THE LIFE OF LOVE

IN THE FOOTSTEPS OF THE LITTLE FLOWER

THE WAY of Spiritual Childhood is not a novel doctrine, and it does not stem from man. It is found in the Gospels: "Amen I say to you, unless you be converted, and become as little children, you shall not enter into the kingdom of heaven."[1] "Suffer the little children to come unto Me, and forbid them not; for of such is the kingdom of God. Amen I say to you, whosoever shall not receive the kingdom of God as a little child, shall not enter into it."[2] "Whosoever therefore shall humble himself as this little child, he is the greater in the kingdom of heaven."[3] "I confess to Thee, O Father, Lord of heaven and earth, because Thou hast hid these things from the wise and prudent, and hast revealed them to little ones. Yea, Father; for so hath it seemed good in Thy sight."[4]

The entire Magnificat is but an exaltation of the spiritual lowliness of the one upon whose lips the Church places the words, "Rejoice with me all you who love the Lord, for, being very small, I have pleased the Most High."[5]

---
1. Matthew 18:3.
2. Mark 10:14-15.
3. Matthew 18:4.
4. Matthew 11:25-26.
5. From the Liturgy.

And when Saint Paul writes, "The foolish things of the world hath God chosen, that He may confound the wise; and the weak things of the world hath God chosen, that He may confound the strong,"[6] is he not eulogizing spiritual childhood? So also Saint Peter when he exhorts the Christians, "As newborn babes, desire the rational milk without guile, that thereby you may grow unto salvation."[7]

To little Saint Teresa of the Child Jesus must go the credit for having understood this particular point in the divine Master's teaching better than anyone else before her. She applied it to the entire spiritual life and by her own example demonstrated to the world its practical application.

So much has already been written and said, both authoritatively and wisely, of how this spiritual life brings about the sanctification of souls and fulfills the needs of our times, (we allude here particularly to the pronouncements of Pope Benedict XV and Pope Pius XI), that any elaboration on our part would be both superfluous and presumptuous. Facts speak more loudly than words in its support; for who could count the souls whom the holy Carmelite nun has won to God, or those who have sanctified themselves by following her Little Way of Love?

Sister Consolata is one of these.

It was her reading of *The Story of a Soul* which captivated her when, as a young woman, she was all eagerness to give herself to God, but could not decide upon which road to follow. She writes in her autobiographical notes:

"One day during the summer of 1924 my friend Gina Richetto asked me to keep a book for her; she would be pass-

---

6. I Corinthians 1:27-28.
7. I Peter 2:2.

ing by later to pick it up. I opened it . . . it was *The Story of a Soul*. After supper I ascended to the mezzanine which overlooks our store[8] and there, by the light of the street lamp, I began to read the life of the Little Flower. A new agitation seized me as I devoured the pages. I came to realize that I was precisely that weak soul whom the Lord had found: 'If the impossible were to happen and Thou wert able to find a soul still weaker than my own. . .' But what attracted me irresistibly was the invitation to little souls, the life of love, and that exclamation 'I wish to love Jesus so much! I wish to love Him as no one has ever yet loved Him!' At that moment something sweet and gentle descended into my soul, something tender and strong. With my face buried in my hands, I listened to the divine call which made itself heard in my heart, powerfully, earnestly. . ."

The voice of grace was urging Pierina to dispel every doubt concerning her religious vocation and was showing her soul the way: the Little Way of Love. Nor was this a case of a simple and passing impulse, but the profound action of grace, as Jesus Himself explicitly confirmed to her on November 27th, 1935:

Little Saint Teresa once wrote: 'Why is it not given to me, O Jesus, to relate Thine ineffable condescension to all little souls? I have a feeling that if the impossible were to happen and Thou wert able to find a soul still weaker than my own, it would please Thee to heap upon her still greater favors, if only that soul would abandon herself with complete faith to Thine infinite mercy.'

Well, I have found that still weaker soul who has abandoned herself with complete faith to My infinite mercy: it

---

8. The Betrone family was at that time operating a grocery store on the Corso Vittorio Emanuele.

is you, Consolata, and through you I will perform marvels which will far exceed your fondest desires![9]

Sister Consolata is therefore one of the conquests of the Little Flower, for she was won over by her to the Little Way of Love; God chose her to confirm that doctrine and to give it a practical form.

THE SELFSAME SPIRIT

It is true that Sister Consolata was the recipient of some extraordinary favors such as the vision of the Blessed Virgin, a prophetic revelation concerning her father's illness, enlightenment as to her own future mission, and the mysterious wound of love which appeared after she had offered herself as a victim-soul. We are dealing here with gratuitous divine gifts which the soul cannot refuse, just as it must not seek after them. The soul must assign them their just value with regard to her own sanctification without becoming inordinately attached to them. That is precisely how Sister Consolata acted: so long as she was favored with them, she felt herself profoundly humiliated and unworthy: later on, when these favors were withdrawn, she was not perturbed thereby, nor did she waver by ever so little from her heroic fidelity to grace.

Instead, we encounter in her life all the characteristics of spiritual childhood, and especially the most essential one, the life of love. It may be well to recall at this point certain thoughts which Saint Teresa of Lisieux expressed in this connection, such as: "Jesus has no need of our works; the one

---

9. She longed to love God, to sanctify herself, and to save souls as will be seen further on.

thing He asks for is our love...'[10] I know of only one thing that I can do: to love Thee, O Jesus! ... To perform great deeds is denied me; I cannot preach the Gospel or shed my blood. But no matter. My Brothers labor on my behalf, while I, poor girl, stand close to the royal throne and offer up love on behalf of those who do battle... Yes, my Jesus, I love Thee! I love the Church, and I bear in mind that the very smallest act of pure love is more useful than all other works taken together."[11]

Now let us follow this up with a page from the pen of Sister Consolata which is not unworthy to be placed on a level with those of her spiritual sister:

"This morning (August 2nd, 1935) I asked myself, 'Why is it, O Jesus, that Thou dost give Thyself with such great tenderness to little souls and surround them with such solicitude, making provision for them in the most minute details ... Why?' And then my soul was enlightened. After Our Lord's words in the Holy Gospel, 'Suffer the little children to come unto Me, and forbid them not; for of such is the kingdom of God,' there occurs a word which reveals Thy parental Heart: 'And embracing them, and laying His hands upon them, He blessed them.'[12] Not only didst Thou bless them but, giving free reign to Thy divine Heart, Thou didst embrace them!

"Thereupon I beheld the great human family as in a spiritual picture. The older children labor and earn their living, and if they are good, they are the pride of their parents; but it is the littlest ones who actually do nothing but love, who occupy the greatest part of the mother's heart.

---
10. We shall see later, in what sense these words are to be understood.
11. Saint Teresa here makes the words of Saint John of the Cross her own.
12. Mark 10:14 and 16.

Now tell me, O Jesus, which gives a mother greater delight: when her son honors her with the successful completion of his studies, or when as an infant he was entirely hers and she could dress and undress him, caress him to her heart's delight, and shower him with all manner of affection? . . . Indeed, it is impossible to express in words the joy which a mother feels at the side of her dear infant's crib! Nor can one tell who feels the greater delight: the child who receives such caresses or the mother who lavishes them upon him. For her infant she desires the most beautiful little clothes, the most delightful things, and if it were possible for that child to remain always a child, the mother would continue to her life's end to devote every care and affection to it without ever tiring of it.

"If we now carry this reasoning over into the spiritual field, we seem to have a perfect illustration of what Jesus does with little souls. They are His own, entirely His own, and He clothes them with parental solicitude in the most beautiful virtues. And as they, like children, accept everything, He can clothe them with virtues or strip them as He pleases. He can press them to His Heart, or leave them in a corner; they remain equally content, so long as they may love Him, so long as He smiles upon them, and so long as they may offer Him something to aid Him in saving souls. The greatest joy which it is possible to taste on earth is to possess God, God alone. Then one delights in an anticipated paradise. And little souls do taste this. . ."

Among such little souls must be counted not only the innocent souls such as the Little Flower, but also those who wish to make reparation and compensate for wasted time. Sister Consolata takes pains to point this out, and counts herself among the latter.

"How good Jesus is! With parental care He carries in His divine arms those who long to keep themselves small in His sight! He bends down to them to satisfy their every desire and wish, even if these souls, like Consolata, are rich only in desires and have had the great misfortune of having offended the Lord! . . . Only Jesus knows how to forget all, indeed He delights in pouring out His graces in superabundance precisely where before there was a superabundance of faults." "Where sin abounded, grace did more abound."[13]

Such was in fact the case of Sister Consolata, and so it will be with all souls, both innocent and sinful, who wish to follow her on that same path of love. In order to illustrate her enthusiasm for a holy spiritual childhood we give here a few anecdotes from her Capuchin convent life which breathe the spirit of the Seraphic Father and possess the fragrance of his Fioretti.

"One day a novice came to my cell to ask for sandals.[14] I pointed out to her that, not being used to them, they would hurt her feet for the first few days. But she replied. 'No, Sister, we are poor folk at home, poor working people. I could not afford to go about always in sandals, so in the winter I used to wear wooden sabots.' She told me this with such evident humility that I was touched. Had I been wealthy, I would have given her a quantity of sandals! . . . Some time later I saw her at the door of the choir, as is our custom during the novena to Saint Francis, begging for an alms of prayer that grace might be given her to draw profit from the spiritual exercises. She asked so humbly, so imploringly, and yet so full of confidence, that I could not resist

---

13. Romans 5:20.
14. Besides Sister Consolata's numerous other duties, she was also the community's cobbler.

whispering to her: 'Yes, I will pray the Lord to make you a great saint!' On that day I came to understand why the Heart of Jesus inclines with such compassionate condescension towards the little ones, the humble souls. It is because our very weakness captivates Him; He is unable to resist the appeal of our wretchedness, and being rich, He gives all manner of 'sandals'!

"One afternoon I seated myself on a bench near the vegetable garden for a few minutes' rest, when the pullets, thinking I was going to feed them, quickly surrounded me, flew up into my lap, and lined themselves along the back of the bench. I thought of our Father Francis, and did not disturb them; but then I felt the urge to lend them my heart so that they too might be able to love as I longed to love. . . One of the pullets had remained in my lap, and I tried to caress it; but it took fright and its little heart began to beat violently. To calm it, I pressed it close, quite close to my heart until it became quiet; it seemed to take pleasure in it and became calm; but then I let it rejoin its companions, and I returned to the choir to adore Jesus. . . I did not give the insignificant occurrence any more thought, but grace explained it to me: if Consolata felt compassion for that little pullet and felt the need of pressing it to her heart to calm it, merely because it was frightened, how much more does the Heart of Jesus, which is a human heart, feel compassion for my poor soul and feel the need to press me to His divine Heart! I had committed a fault against charity that morning, and so felt unworthy of such love, but another thought comforted me: what merit did that little pullet have that I should have come to press it to my heart and caress it? None whatever. Compassion had merely urged me to do it. Well then, it was that same compassion which drove

Jesus toward my poor soul. O Jesus, I am Thy little pullet! And so it seemed only natural to go up close to His Heart and to continue to love Him there.

"Jesus is truly at our disposal here among us Capuchin nuns, and one lives near His tabernacle in indescribable familiarity. This must please Jesus, for when we approach Him in our private prayers and devotions, He floods our beings and lets us feel His divine presence in an especially intimate and affectionate way. . . Somehow it always used to seem a bit pharisaical to me to go up close to the tabernacle to pray, when I ought rather to imitate the poor publican of the Gospel. But the delightful picture of Jesus caressing the children drove away all fear, and I came to understand that not only has the soul a need to pray close to the Living Jesus, but the divine Heart of Jesus delights in having us near Him without much ceremony, like the children in the picture who rival one another in seeing who can press the closest to Him."

WHAT JESUS PREFERS

Jesus not infrequently intervened in person to confirm Sister Consolata in these sentiments and in the matter of spiritual childhood. In the intellectual visions with which she was favored, when Jesus pressed her to His divine Heart, she would always see herself, or rather her soul, under the image of a very young child. Beyond these there were also certain divine instructions, and for these we quote Sister Consolata's own words:

"During my first years with the Capuchin nuns I gave expression to my love for Jesus solely' by working hard in

His cause; but even before the spiritual exercises connected with my first vows Jesus told me: *You trouble yourself about many things; but only one thing is necessary, to love Me!*"[15]

Jesus here states specifically in what this "one thing necessary" consists: love. And that applies equally to the contemplative life and to the active or mixed life, all considerations aside as to which of these might be intrinsically more excellent than the other. In practice, in Sister Consolata's own case, it does not mean that hard work is in itself opposed to the life of love, but natural activities must not throttle the interior life.

"While I was making my meditation in choir on Whitsunday, 1931, Jesus asked me to make the following vow: 'O Jesus, I have vowed to Thee, and I firmly believe, **that the path to be followed by me is the Way of Love. To this I abandon myself completely and confidently** and, while canceling all previous intentions and trusting in Thee, I promise Thee to live for love from to-day on and until my last breath, offering Thee one unceasing act of love, accomplishing everything with love, and searching for nothing but love!'

"I had thus been shown the path which I was to follow, and I found myself now fully enlightened. I came to understand that Jesus Himself wished to work in my soul. . . I understood then that it was more needful for me to love than to think. . ."[16]

"Yes, an unceasing act of love! That alone and nothing else; for love is everything, and in the practice of this love all other virtues are practiced.[17]

---

15. "Martha, Martha, thou art careful, and art troubled about many things: but one thing is necessary. Mary hath chosen the better part, which shall not be taken away from her." (Luke 10:41-42).

16. This will be more fully explained further on.

17. Works in themselves do not do honor to God, but the spirit which prompts

SPIRITUAL CHILDHOOD AND THE LIFE OF LOVE 25

"During May, 1935 a newly appointed regular confessor began his holy ministry among us and at one of my first confessions told me: 'Overcome one defect each week,[18] then you will make good confessions, and you will delight the Heart of Jesus.' I received that advice with joy and concentrated all my efforts on overcoming one defect each week. But in my preoccupation to finish the week without having spoken a useless word or had an idle thought, etc., I gave no more thought to love,[19] so that the Blessed Virgin one day said to me: 'You lose yourself in so many trifles, and you do not give to Jesus the one thing He asks for; in your last hour you will desire in vain to live longer and to perform one more act of love. It will then be too late!' I understood, and applied myself anew to love.[20]

"One evening during my meditation I was seized by a violent emotion, and a voice which pretended to be divine foretold for me pains, sorrows, and sufferings. 'Your hour

---

them; that is why Jesus in the Gospel censures the works of piety and penance which are performed for the sake of ostentation. (Luke 6:23). "Every other iniquity," writes Saint Augustine, "grows out of the performance of evil deeds; pride, on the other hand, attempts to seduce even the good works themselves so as to bring them to naught." (*Letters*, 211, No. 6). The soul who lives for love guards herself well against such insidious dangers and avoids every risk of defiling the good works she performs. This is why the spirit of spiritual childhood is so pleasing to God.

18. In the *Imitation of Christ* (I, 11, 5) we read: "If each year we were to extirpate one vice, we would quickly become men of perfection." The advice of Sister Consolata's new confessor does not only differ as to the length of time, but also in its spirit.

19. She means to say: "I thought no more about loving with an actual love, that is, with the unceasing act of love." Habitual charity expresses itself in performing the daily tasks, and in so doing it builds up, that is, creates, positive energies and purifies them.

20. "If we hold that the benefit of religion lies solely in these exterior observances, our devotion will quickly come to an end." (*Imitation of Christ*, I, 2, 4). Sister Consolata is slowly discovering the classical outline of the spiritual life; and divine enlightenment is guiding her toward that interior liberation from the instrumental complexity of perfection, in order to raise her to what is essential in it, that is charity. (See Saint Thomas, II, II, 184, 3).

has come . . . and what have you done so far for souls? Nothing! . . .' At that I abandoned myself to the divine will, and regained my peace. I rejected that voice by remembering what Jesus had told me, and I soon discovered the enemy's trick by which he had hoped to draw me away from my simple way of love.

"Now I am completely happy: I feel I am on the right road, the very one which Jesus desires of me. There remains but one thing for me to do: to live this life of love, even to die of love! . . . Yes, my Jesus, I know that what Thou desirest of me is love, nothing but love. To follow any other road would be to deceive myself and to lose time."

WHAT PLEASES JESUS

Jesus Himself manifested His satisfaction from time to time that Sister Consolata was maintaining herself in the spirit and state of spiritual childhood. Without a doubt she received from God great gifts and extraordinary graces. But why? Jesus Himself supplied the answer, and it is of such a nature as to dissipate the doubts which some persons might entertain concerning this soul, as though she had not merited the divine gifts because she too had her shortcomings. Such thoughts spring from an erroneous opinion regarding these freely given graces or charisma as Saint Paul calls them. Jesus explained on December 15th, 1935:

Look, Consolata, people are accustomed to measure the virtue of a soul by the graces which I grant her, but they deceive themselves, for I am free to act as I please. For example, does your virtue merit the great graces which I have granted you? Poor Consolata, you have no virtue, you have no merits, you have nothing![21] *You would have your sins, but they exist no more, for I have forgotten them for all eternity. Why then so many, many graces for you in particular? Because I am free to do good to whom I will. The little ones are My weakness—that explains everything!* . . . *And no one can accuse Me of injustice, for a sovereign is free to bestow his royal favors on whom he will.*[22]

On March 19th, 1935, Jesus favored Sister Consolata with a great revelation concerning the sanctity of Saint Joseph. Astounded and deeply moved, the humble maiden turned to Him:

"Why, O Jesus, dost Thou tell me all these things, to me who can do nothing, and why dost Thou conceal them from the great ones who might be able to do so much?"

Jesus replied: *To the little ones I tell everything.*

Our Lord also deigned to foretell to Sister Consolata many things about her future apostolate after death. Confused over so much condescension she one day complained to Him that He was telling her too much; but Jesus answered on December 12th, 1935:

You feel that I am telling you too much about your future? . . . *That I tell you everything?* . . . *You are quite right, but what can one do when the heart is overflowing?* . . . *And besides, you are so little that you are content to write it all down, and it is My wish that you should put everything in writing, and so I can tell you everything.*

---

21. "Who distinguishes thee? Or what hast thou that thou hast not received? And if thou hast received, why dost thou glory, as if you hadst not received it?" (I Cor. 4:7).

22. "All these things one and the same Spirit worketh, dividing to everyone according as He will." (I Cor. 12:11).

Have you ever noticed that when a mother is caressing and fondling her youngest infant, she will tell him many things which she would not tell to one of her older children? . . . Her maternal heart has need to expand and to tell that little creature who does not yet understand but merely smiles up at her, all the plans which she treasures for his future. She will tell him everything, truly everything, just as I am now doing with you. But note that when that child begins to talk and someone asks him, who made his lovely little dress, he will reply quite happily 'my mamma,' and he will delight in possessing that dress and the admiration it calls forth.

Do you notice the difference between great souls and little souls? The latter enjoy the virtues with which they feel themselves adorned because it is God who has bestowed them; but the former conceal them for fear that, having labored in pursuit of them, they might lose them through pride.[23]

Do you understand, Consolata? . . . That is why I tell everything to little souls; they deprive Me of nothing; they direct all praise, honor, and glory to Me alone.

This was not the first time that Jesus used the analogy of the child and its little dress to point out how little souls abandon themselves with confidence to the workings of grace for their own sanctification. They are content merely

---

23. This stresses the active part of the soul in the pursuit of perfection; little souls place the emphasis on grace and the gifts of God, whereas great souls, while supporting themselves by grace, place the emphasis on freedom and the cultivation of virtues; the former enjoy the love of God, the latter practice humility. The analogy with the dress manifestly recalls the clothing with virtues; infused at baptism, the Christian virtues are activated through the acquired virtues which presuppose man's freedom of action in order to live in honesty and in beauty.

to assist grace in everything with the utmost docility. Jesus told Sister Consolata on October 8th, 1935:

Consolata, I delight in you because I can do everything I wish, and it is I who am doing everything. You know with what care and affection a mother makes a little dress for her infant; she really puts her whole heart into it. But if the child were not to let her make the dress because he wanted to make it himself, that would sadden the mother.[24]

Sister Consolata understood that divine language well, and so will all souls who have "a simple and straightforward faith."[25] It will also be well to bear in mind what Jesus declared to her on November 9th, 1935, concerning divine locutions:

If I ask you to write it down, it is because My words will bear much fruit. My reasoning may at times seem childish to you, but that is because I adapt My words to you who are so little; but remember that any word of Mine is spirit, is light!

We ought not to be astonished at the way in which Jesus treats little souls. Saint Francis de Sales observes that "God is innocent with the innocent, kind toward the kind, loving toward those who are loving, tender toward those who are tender, and at times He is carried away by love to treat with divine caresses those souls who out of love for purity make themselves little children in His sight."

But even when Jesus adapts His speech to the smallness of the creature, His words are in truth always "spirit and life"

---

24. All this will be better explained further on when we speak of the love of abandonment.

25. In the sense that such a faith must rest upon the authority of the Church, which alone has the duty to authenticate the various divine manifestations of which we speak here.

on account of the precious concepts of spiritual life which they contain. At the end of a certain day which had been filled with extremely arduous work, so that it had hindered her in the continuity of her love, Sister Consolata asked pardon of Jesus for having been overwhelmed by so much work; but Our Lord comforted her:

You must know that what would constitute a fault in great souls is not one in little souls; and you are so very small! I have made it all good! I have been loving on your behalf, and so I count your entire day as one continuous act of love.

Another time, when she was praying for the success of a series of sermons which her spiritual director was preaching, Jesus told her on October 16th, 1935:

Yes. This preaching will bear abundant fruit for eternal life. To little souls I concede everything! You deny Me nothing, so I deny you nothing!

Concerning her calling to be a victim-soul, Jesus gave her this assurance on November 13th, 1935:

Remember always that My strength will never fail you. Of all the virtues which I grant you, I endow you in particular with this one, for you are weakness itself!

It was the way of spiritual childhood therefore which drew down the favor of the Most High upon Sister Consolata. Not only did she sense herself to be small and make herself of no account, but she felt herself utterly insignificant in the sight of God; it was this innermost recognition of her own weakness which brought her to hope for everything from Jesus working within her.

- II -

THE LIFE OF LOVE AND CHRISTIAN VIRTUES

HAVE FAITH IN LOVE

IN ITS essence the way of spiritual childhood consists in a life of love, and the first requisite for practicing this life of love with conviction and fruitfulness is to believe in Love.

This means above all to believe that God is Love, "Deus charitas est."[1] *'You cannot live without love,'* Our Lord once told Saint Catherine of Genoa, *'because I, your God, am Love.'* And in his comments on the Canticles Saint Bernard writes: "This Bridegroom is not only the Lover; He is Love Itself,"[2] and he continues: "Love is a great thing, provided always that it is directed to its Source, that it returns to its origin, and is carried back to its well-spring, so as to draw from it and flow ever more abundantly." In order that this condition might really verify itself, Christ Jesus comes to us as the Redeemer and Restorer, and from that fact "we have known and have believed the charity which God hath to us,"[3] that He loves us, and that in fact He is Love Itself.

---
1. I John 4:16.
2. In Cant. 83:4.
3. I John 4:16.

Belief in this fundamental truth is necessary in order that the soul may perceive in love the primal and efficient cause of all the works of God. It was the superabundance of God's love which drove Him to become the Creator; His love inspired the Incarnation: "God so loved the world as to give His only-begotten Son,"[4] and the Redemption: "I live in the faith of the Son of God, who loved me, and delivered Himself for me;"[5] His love gave us the Eucharist and the other sacraments: "Having loved His own who were in the world, He loved them unto the end;"[6] His love created purgatory for those souls who had not been sufficiently purified by the trials of this life; His love prepared an abode of peace for souls of good will; and the abuse of His love and unbelief in it created hell.[7] Saint Francis de Sales has justly written: "In the Church of Jesus Christ everything is at the service of love, everything is founded upon love, everything is love."[8]

But it is also necessary to turn from contemplating the great works of God to discern the wise touch of the Hand of God and the imprint of His Love in the particular happenings in the world and in the life of the individual. God can perform naught but works of love; His thoughts, His acts, His every divine desire is love, even when it castigates. Sister Consolata writes:

". . . On the evening of August 25th, 1934, I was in my cell near the window. I had been given a book to read and paging through it, I read of the punishments which Our

---

4. John 3:16.
5. Galatians, 2:20.
6. John 13:1.
7. See Dante's *Inferno* 3, 2.
8. *Of the Love of God*, Preface.

Lord threatened. 'O Jesus, why dost Thou desire to wash us in our own blood, which is impure. Wash us rather in Thine!' *'Consolata, look up to heaven. . .'* I looked, and in the marvelous blue discovered a star, the first one of the evening; and while I was contemplating it, Jesus called loudly to my heart: *'Have confidence! . . .'* Meanwhile the lovely vault of heaven was clothing itself with stars, and I became captivated by its mysterious charm: seating myself on the low window sill, I remained absorbed in silent contemplation. It seemed to me that heaven had ceased being displeased with the earth, and that the peaceful reign of God was spreading over this poor world."

                      ✿   ✿   ✿

Peace to the world, yes, but in the kingdom of God! Jesus is the Saviour of the world; He is able to save it, and He desires to save it.

Consolata, I am in need of victim-souls! The world is going to its ruin, but I wish to save it.

Consolata, the devil one day swore he would ruin you, and I vowed I would save you. . . Satan also swore he would ruin the world, and I vowed I would save it; and I will save it through the triumph of My mercy and My love. Yes, I will save the world through My merciful love! Write this down.

It should be noted that Jesus does not exclude chastisements, for these may be necessary for the salvation of the world and of souls.

Jesus explained this thought on November 15th, 1935, during the economic crisis which gripped the world before the start of the war:

The distress which reigns in the world at the present

time is not the work of My justice, but of My mercy. For fewer sins are being committed because money is scarce, and many more prayers are being raised to heaven by people in financial straits. Do not think that the sorrowful conditions on earth do not move Me; but I love souls; I wish them to be saved; and in order to achieve My end, I am constrained to be severe; but believe Me, I do it out of mercy! During times of abundance souls forget Me and are lost; in times of distress they turn to Me and save themselves. That is indeed the way it happens!

Note the luminous depth of these words which recall the divine instructions to the prophet Isaias: "Woe to the Assyrian, he is the rod and staff of My anger, and My indignation is in their hands."[9] And by the lips of Jeremias, God spoke thus of Babylon: "With thee I will dash nations together, and with thee I will destroy kingdoms."[10] This mystical concept of historic tragedies, which were brought about by heads of nations as mere tools in God's hands, does not lessen their responsibility for the evil they have done and for which they will have to render an account; nor does this prevent the omnipotence of God from having even human wickedness serve to carry out the designs of His Providence for eternal bliss. Thus the scourges of this present life, when accepted and patiently applied to one's own purification, may become means of sanctification and expiation.

And returning to the same thought a few days later, again in response to Sister Consolata's prayers for peace, Our Lord declared on April 29th, 1942:

Pray, pray for humanity in order that I may mitigate

---

9. Isaias 10:5.
10. Jeremias 51:20.

these sorrows and save souls! If I permit so much sorrow in the world, it is for that one purpose, to save souls for eternity. The world is going to perdition, it is hastening to its ruin...

As with public disasters, so it is also with the misfortunes of families and individuals. Always, even in the most desperately sad cases when bewildered humanity is seeking for a reason, the reply from heaven is once again: Love, Goodness, the Mercy of God. One day, when Sister Consolata was grieving over the sudden death of a childhood companion by which four children had been orphaned, the oldest barely nine years old, Jesus replied:

Celeste Canda is now enjoying the beatific vision for all eternity, and from heaven she is watching over the souls of her four children with greater tenderness than if she had remained on earth.

What sweet comfort, what heavenly light, do not these simple words bring to all bereaved families!

To believe in Love, in short, means to believe that Jesus loves us, wishes to save us, and that everything He does or permits, both in the great outer world and in the little world of the soul, is always for our best. Only a few souls, however, even among those dedicated to piety, possess this living and practical faith in Love. If they have it at all, it is weak and vacillates easily under the blows of the chisel with which the divine Artist is intent on perfecting the work of His hands.

Many are the souls who are inclined to see in God a severe Master rather than a kind Father! For such souls is intended Our Lord's sweet lament to Sister Consolata on November 22nd, 1935:

Do not make Me out a God of rigor, whereas I am naught but a God of Love!

For such souls is also the reply which Jesus gave to Sister Consolata's query as to how He preferred to be addressed (September 26th, 1936):

Limitless Love; Infinite Goodness!

For them is also Our Lord's advice to Sister Consolata on July 22nd, 1936, when she was undecided whether to write in a letter "the Most Sacred Heart of Jesus" or "the Gentle Heart of Jesus:"

Write 'the Gentle Heart of Jesus'; for everyone knows that I am holy, but not all know that I am gentle!

The soul, therefore, who desires to live in love, must ground herself well in this truth and apply it to the thousand and one details of everyday life. She must not stop at creatures and events, but must see God and His love in everything. "Oh, what must we not fear," writes Saint Francis de Sales, "and even more, what may we not hope for as children of such a Father, who is so full of goodness, who loves us and wishes us to be saved, and who is so wise as to prepare and apply the means for our salvation? What goodness of will, what foresight in planning! What wisdom in execution!"[11]

Always, in good fortune and under adverse conditions, in peaceful and in stormy times, the soul must keep her forces intact so that the cry of her unshakable faith may reach to heaven: "O Sacred Heart of Jesus, I believe in Thy love for me!" And this is exactly what the Apostle of Love asserted: "And we have known and have believed the charity which God hath to us."[12]

---

11. *Of the Love of God*, 4, 8.
12. I John 4:16.

HOPE IN LOVE

Our faith in Jesus' love for us and our own love for Him raise the soul to a more perfect love, or as Saint Thomas puts it: "Hope is made more perfect through the intervention of Love."[13] "Love hopes for all things."[14] And of hope, as of love, there can never be too much! It is meant for all, for the innocent and for the sinner, but more especially for the latter; for while the compassion of Jesus encompasses every soul, it does so in particular in the case of those who are most in need of His mercy.

Jesus came down from heaven especially for sinners: "I am not come to call the just, but sinners."[15] To them is directed the touching solicitude of the Good Shepherd: "I am the Good Shepherd. . ."[16] "What man of you that hath a hundred sheep; and if he shall lose one of them, doth he not leave the ninety-nine in the desert, and go after that which was lost until he find it?"[17] For them are intended the father's delicate attentions toward the prodigal son: "Bring forth quickly the first robe, and put it on him, and put a ring on his hand, and shoes on his feet: and bring hither the fatted calf, and kill it, and let us eat and make merry: because this my son was dead, and is come to life again: was lost, and is found."[18] No, Christ did not come down from heaven to destroy a soul who was in danger, but to raise her up again; not to humiliate and crush one who had fallen, but to reestablish her in His grace and His love: "that there might be

---

13. II, II, 17, 8.
14. I Corinthians 13:7.
15. Matthew 9:13.
16. John 10:14.
17. Luke 15:4.
18. Luke 15:22-24.

fulfilled what was said by the mouth of the prophet Isaias: 'Behold My Servant whom I have chosen, My Beloved in whom My Soul hath been well pleased... The bruised reed He shall not break; and smoking flax He shall not extinguish... and in His Name the Gentiles shall hope.' "[19]

Nor will God send down the avenging fire desired by the Apostles to consume the erring: "You know not of what spirit you are. The Son of Man came not to destroy souls but to save."[20] Rather will He cause the flame of His merciful love to blaze forth: "I am come to cast fire on the earth: and what will I, but that it be kindled?"[21] With pleasure He shares His bread with sinners, and sits down to table with them: "As He was sitting at meat in the house (of Matthew), behold many publicans and sinners came, and sat down with Jesus and His disciples."[22] Energetically does He defend them from the maligners: "They that are in health need not a physician, but they that are ill. Go then and learn what this meaneth, 'I will have mercy and not sacrifice.' "[23]

When to man's puny heart it seems already much to pardon a brother seven times: "Lord, how often shall my brother offend against me, and I forgive him? Till seven times?"[24] the Heart of Jesus replies: "I say not to thee, till seven times; but till seventy times seven times."[25] Jesus forgives again and again. Never a reproof, never a reproach for guilt! "Woman, where are they that accused thee? Hath no man condemned thee?... Neither will I condemn thee.

---

19. Matthew 12:17-21; Isaias 42:1 ff.
20. Luke 9:55-56.
21. Luke 12:49.
22. Matthew 9:10.
23. Matthew 9:12-13; Osee 6:6.
24. Matthew 18:21.
25. Matthew 18:22.

THE LIFE OF LOVE AND THE CHRISTIAN VIRTUES

Go, and now sin no more."[26] Never does Jesus withhold His divine favors from a repentant sinner. Even though Peter denied Him, he nevertheless receives the keys of the kingdom of heaven; Paul, the persecutor, becomes the apostle of nations; the great sinner in the Gospel is rescued from the street and becomes a saint; thus it is true that "there shall be joy in heaven upon one sinner that doth penance, more than upon ninety-nine just who need not penance."[27]

* * *

Sister Consolata's mission is precisely this, to point out to the world how limitless is the mercy of the Sacred Heart of Jesus, first to her Brothers and Sisters whom she has spiritually adopted, and then to all souls. She can demonstrate not only with words but with facts how much Jesus has done in her own soul to make her one of the finest products of His grace.

She modeled her heart upon that of Jesus, and always felt a lively compassion for poor sinners and an ardent desire to lead them all back to the Heart of God.

". . . At times Jesus pours out His Heart to me and laments over some soul. When I then persuade Him that matters are not really so bad and I make indulgent excuses, I feel within me that Jesus brightens up and is content; and I end up by praying for that soul. The Heart of Jesus is like a mother's. When a mother is overcome by some sorrow which an ungrateful son has caused her and confides in a close friend, and when the latter then puts her son in a better light to comfort her, oh how that mother delights in

---
26. John 8:10-11.
27. Luke 15:7.

the thought that her boy is still good! She has need to think and believe in that way. A mother's heart is but a weak reflection of the divine Heart! A mother, however, is unable to transform the heart of an ungrateful son; whereas Jesus will, if we but ask Him, convert the unfaithful soul who wounds His Heart."

Thus she wrote on December 5th, 1935. Two days later, as though to prove to her that such thoughts came from Him and corresponded to the goodness of His divine Heart, Jesus Himself confirmed them almost verbatim:

A true mother will not consider her child ugly, no matter how much it may be so; to her it is always lovely, and so it will always remain in her innermost heart. That is precisely the way My Heart feels toward souls: though they be ugly, soiled, filthy, My Love considers them always beautiful. I suffer when their ugliness is confirmed to Me; on the other hand, I rejoice when, in conformity with My parental sentiments, someone dissuades Me about their ugliness and tells Me that it is not true and that they are still beautiful. The souls are Mine; for them I have given all My Blood!

Now do you understand how much My parental Heart is wounded by every severe judgment, reprimand, or condemnation, even though based on truth, and how much comfort, on the other hand, is afforded Me by every act of compassion, indulgence and mercy? You must never judge anyone; never say a harsh word against anyone; instead, console My Heart, distract Me from My sorrow; with eager charity make Me see only the good side of a guilty soul. I will believe you, and then I will hear your prayer in her favor and will grant it. If you only knew how I suffer when I must dispense justice! You see, My Heart needs to be comforted; It wishes to dispense mercy, not justice!

Such divine words may appear novel and may even cause astonishment if only considered superficially. It is not meant here that in the eyes of Jesus a sinful soul as such could ever seem beautiful; but a soul always appears beautiful when seen through the eyes of the infinite Love which has created her, redeemed her, and desires to see her saved. Similarly, it is not meant that Jesus would wish to be, or could ever be, deceived by a sinful soul, but that He takes pleasure in being piously deceived by just souls who interpose themselves between Himself and sinners to excuse them and as it were conceal them behind their own love of reparation; in doing so they follow the example which He Himself gave from the Cross when He interposed Himself between God the Father and guilty humanity: "Father, forgive them, for they know not what they do!"[28] In other words, having in the Gospel proclaimed the blessedness of the merciful, God has by that very fact revealed His infinite happiness in always showing mercy. On the other hand, His mercy can show itself only in the face of misery—and what misery could be greater than sin?

According to Saint Thomas Aquinas, sin does not destroy the "bonum naturae," so that God's image remains in man even after sin, though "obscured and disfigured."[29] This reflection of the divine image is the open door to regeneration and the hope of pardon, it lets the light of Jesus the Saviour shine into the darkness of sin, and so gives a "new and original" concept of man.

---

28. Luke 23:34.
29. I, II, 85, 2, and I, 93, 8 ad. 3.

Goodness and mercy are poured out upon all men by the Sacred Heart of Jesus, but in particular upon sinners as having the greater need: "They that are well have no need of a physician, but they that are sick."[30] That is what Jesus said in the Gospel, and He confirmed it to Sister Consolata:

Consolata, you must never forget that I always am, and love to be, kind and merciful toward My creatures. The mercy which I exercise toward poor sinners in life consists in heaping benefits upon them.

○   ○   ○

Other similar manifestations of the merciful Heart of Jesus will be met with further on in this book which is but a lesson of love for the just and an invitation to love for sinners. We cannot forego inserting at this point, however, another page which was dictated by the Sacred Heart of Jesus to Sister Consolata; it will afford great comfort by reviving hope in sinners and in those souls also who suffer from an excessive and at times oppressive fear of not being able to attain to eternal salvation. This lack of Christian hope, besides being harmful to the soul, also offends the Sacred Heart in Its merciful love and Its desire to save. On December 15th, 1935, Jesus instructed Sister Consolata to write thus for the benefit of all souls:

Consolata, it often happens that good and pious souls, and very frequently also souls who are consecrated to Me, wound My Heart to Its very depths by some diffident phrase such as: 'Who knows whether I will be saved?'

Open the Gospel and read there My promises. I promised to My sheep: 'I will give them life everlasting; and they shall not perish forever, and no man shall pluck them

---

30. Mark 2:17.

*out of My Hand.'*³¹ *Do you understand, Consolata? No one can take a soul from Me! Now read on: 'That which My Father hath given Me, is greater than all; and no one can snatch them out of the Hand of My Father.'*³² *Do you understand, Consolata? No one can snatch a soul from Me. . . In all eternity they will not perish . . . because I give them eternal life. For whom have I spoken these words? For all the sheep, for all souls!*³³ *Why then the insult, 'who knows whether I will be saved?' I have given assurances in the Gospel that no one can pluck a soul from Me and that I will give that soul eternal life, and so the soul cannot perish. Believe Me, Consolata, into hell go only those who really wish to go there; for though no one can snatch a soul from Me, the soul may, through the free will granted her, flee from Me, may betray Me, deny Me, and so go to Satan of her own volition.*

*Oh, if instead of wounding My Heart with such distrust, you would give a little more thought to the heaven which awaits you! I did not create you for hell but for heaven, not as a companion for the devil but to enjoy Me in everlasting love!*³⁴ *You see, Consolata, to hell go only those who wish to go there. . . How foolish is your fear of being damned!*³⁵ *After having shed My Blood in order to save your soul, after*

---

31. John 10:28.
32. John 10:29.
33. Our Divine Saviour "will have all men to be saved, and to come to the knowledge of the truth." (I Tim. 2:4).
34. Even though a healthy fear of hell may serve to detach a soul from sin, the hope of attaining to the Supreme Goodness can induce a soul to put the precious talent of grace to work more effectively in acts of virtue. Hence the need of bringing souls to hope by means of love, for "love precedes hope; one hopes only for that good which one loves. . ." (*Of the Love of God*, I, 4). "Hope is a love which waits and aspires." (*Of the Love of God*, II, 16).
35. Jesus refers here to the excessive and unjustified fear which sometimes oppresses even pious souls.

having surrounded your soul with graces upon graces all through your entire existence . . . would I permit Satan, My worst enemy, to rob Me of that soul at the last moment of her life, just when I am about to gather in the fruit of the Redemption and when therefore that soul is on the point of loving Me forever? Would I do that, when in the Holy Gospel I have promised to give the soul eternal life and that no one can snatch her from My Hands? Consolata, how is it possible to believe such a monstrosity?

You see, final impenitence is found only in a soul who purposely wishes to go to hell and therefore obstinately refuses My mercy, for I never refuse to pardon anyone! I offer the gift of My immense compassion to all, for My Blood was shed for all, for all! No, it is not the multiplicity of sins which condemns a soul, for I forgive everything if she repents, but it is the obstinacy of not wishing to be pardoned, of wishing to be damned![36] *Dismas on the cross had only one single act of faith in Me, but many, many sins; he was pardoned in an instant, however, and on the very day of his repentance he entered into My kingdom and is a saint! Behold the triumph of My mercy and of faith in Me!*

No, Consolata, My Father who has given Me the souls is greater and more powerful than all the demons! No one can snatch souls from the Hand of My Father!

O Consolata, have confidence in Me! Trust Me always! You must have a blind confidence that I will fulfill all the great promises which I have made you, for I am kind, immensely kind and merciful, and 'I desire not the death of the wicked, but that the wicked turn from his way, and live.'[37]

---

36. Such obstinacy makes men equal to demons. (*Saint Thomas*, III, Suppl. 99, 3).
37. Ezechiel 33:11.

To God's willingness to grant salvation must therefore correspond a willingness on the part of the sinner to live, that is, to save himself through his conversion to God. "I will arise and go to my father."[38] This truth is expressed so clearly, repeatedly and vigorously by Ezechiel that he is rightly called "the prophet of human responsibility" in the "new and original" sense of God's doctrine about man.

Sister Consolata responded fully to these divine invitations. She was not spared temptations in this connection, but she always came out of them victoriously. Let us quote from her writings on November 3rd, 1935:

"One night at Matins I was deeply impressed by the passage in the Gospel concerning the man who had planted a fig tree in his vineyard.[39] I copied the passage upon returning to my cell and made some notes on it for my day of retreat. It seemed to me that this was the history of my own soul: if you will bear fruit, good; if not, I will cut you down... The fear of divine judgment assailed me vehemently and opened up an abyss between God the Father and my own faithless soul. I wept and did not dare raise my eyes to heaven any more; . . . everything seemed irrevocably lost. What an hour of torture and anguish! . . . What could I offer up to placate that justice? What could I promise, when each new day merely proved my own infidelity? . . . At last I gathered all my strength of soul and cried out: 'Jesus, I place my trust in Thee!' And behold, a bridge appeared to span that fearful abyss...[40] Trust in Jesus re-united this poor crea-

---

38. Luke 15:18.
39. Luke 13:6-9.
40. The image of the bridge recalls the identical teaching of Saint Catherine of Siena in her *Dialogue on Divine Providence,* chapter 21.

ture with her Supreme Creator high above all her anguish . . . and peace returned. Confidence in God! That alone gives me wings; fear freezes me and paralyzes every activity. . ."

Sister Consolata had the same experience again during the Holy Hour on the night preceding the First Friday of July 1936:

". . . I chose my inspirational quotation at random, approached close to the tabernacle, and read: 'Our Lord has loved you and has given Himself to you without reserve, and will you still divide your affections?' It was an hour of Gethsemane! Divine Love and its manifestations humiliated me profoundly. I have been almost overwhelmed by God's gifts, by the affection which the Heart of Jesus showers upon me. No, more than that a God certainly could not do for His creature; Jesus could not love me more than that! And I, how have I responded? . . . My unfaithfulness in keeping silence appeared to me in all its monstrosity; no, I was not loving God without reserve; I was not giving Him everything; or, as soon as I did, I would take it back. My God, what ingratitude! . . . The load crushed and all but annihilated me; Justice reproached me. In that great anguish I thought there remained nothing but to cast myself with full confidence into the Heart of Jesus which is good, infinitely good! . . . Was Jesus waiting for that act? . . . Peace returned, and love! . . ."

Sister Consolata also had to pass through other no less painful trials, since she had offered herself to suffer hell upon earth in order to save her poor Brothers from eternal damnation. But she was heroically able to keep true to her vow which the Divine Father had one day asked of her in preparation as it were for the great assaults which awaited her (October 8th, 1934):

Honor God with your confidence. Swear to Me that you will always believe, no matter in what state your soul may find herself, that there is a heaven open to you!

She had also on several occasions received a formal promise from Jesus that she would go directly to heaven without passing through purgatory. Thus, on September 19th, 1935:

No, Consolata, we will not go to purgatory; we will pass from the cell to paradise!

And even earlier, in response to her fears on this point, because of the sins she had committed:

Listen, Consolata, if the good thief, in addition to all his own, had also committed all your faults, do you suppose I would have changed My verdict?

"Oh no, Jesus, Thou wouldst have said just the same: 'To-day thou shalt be with Me in paradise!'"

Well then, some evening I will say the same words to you!

TRUST IN LOVE

Confidence is the flower of Christian hope,[41] for not only does it make us strive with a happy spirit toward the heavenly fatherland, but it makes us proceed with speed and without halting on the path to holiness. Love and confidence are therefore the wings with which the soul undertakes the most daring flights and victoriously gains every height. If confidence wanes, then love also languishes, and the soul

---

41. Confidence presupposes a certain vigor in hoping. (Saint Thomas II, II, 129, 6).

merely drags herself along. In fact, lack of faith is the greatest obstacle to the divine workings in a soul outside of self-seeking.

In most cases we lack trust in God because we have too much confidence in ourselves. Then, when the soul experiences her own inability to do good, she grieves beyond measure and is greatly perturbed. The very opposite ought to be the case; it is because of its very weakness that the infant has the right to be sustained by his mother, and the same thing happens in the spiritual field; it is our own extreme weakness which gives us the right to count on God's strength; our countless needs are what attract the tender Heart of Jesus. That is an important point in the battle for sanctity: our every imperfection, whether more or less voluntary, should become our point of support for raising our confidence ever higher. A love which does not trust, is no more love, but fear; and every anguish which is caused by a lack of confidence in God dishonors and wounds the Heart of God.

This is the reason why we find the phrase "honor God with your confidence" repeated several times by God the Father and by Jesus in their converse with Sister Consolata. One day (September 17th, 1935), she confided to Jesus:

"O Jesus, the fact that Thou dost speak to my poor soul, that Thou dost deign to instruct me, that ought to be the greatest joy of my heart; but instead, I am constrained to remain almost silent because my poverty is so great; there is really nothing that could attract Thy divine glance toward me; and because I realize that, a doubt is sometimes born within me: am I not perhaps greatly deceived? . . . Jesus, forgive me! Yes, I do believe that Thou art infinite goodness!" Jesus replied:

THE LIFE OF LOVE AND THE CHRISTIAN VIRTUES

Look, Consolata, your poverty is limited, but My love has no limits!

A few days later, on September 19th, 1935, she exclaimed: "O Jesus, that Thou couldst love the white and spotless lilies, that I can believe; but that Thou shouldst love me . . . that I cannot understand!" And Jesus:

If you will remember that I did not come for the just but for sinners, you will understand at once, Consolata![42]

"One evening," she writes, "I was desolate and was sobbing before the tabernacle: 'Oh Jesus, I am always the same; I promise, and then. . .' And He replied:

I also am always the same and never change! But He said this is such a tone that my desolation was changed into joy: if He was not grieved, why then should I be so distressed?"

This reminder of the immutability of God stresses the need for sinful and unstable creatures to have a solid and permanent support.[43]

Jesus never permitted Sister Consolata to brood over her own failings. On November 2nd, 1935, He told her:

If you should happen to commit some fault, do not grieve over it, but come and place it quickly within My Heart; then strengthen your determination to strive for the opposite virtue, but with great calmness. In that manner your every fault will become a step in advance.[44]

With great calmness . . . for the enemy is astute and proceeds according to a tactical plan. If he is able to in-

---

42. See Matthew 9:13.
43. See Psalm 101:28; Hebrews 1:12.
44. "It can never be said too often: we must repent for our past sins with a steadfast repentance, that is, with one that is composed, constant, and tranquil; not excited, restless, and discouraged." (*Of the Love of God,* Book 9, chapter 7).

oculate a soul with the poison of diffidence, he is well satisfied, for the rest will come by itself. The soul will come to be perturbed, and that is fatal to it, as Jesus explained to Sister Consolata on August 2nd, 1936:

If the soul can keep calm, then she will remain master of herself; but if she is perturbed, then it is easy for her to fall.

Having noticed that Jesus permitted everything except disquiet in her soul, Sister Consolata one day asked Him for the reason; He gave her to understand that a peaceful soul is like a spring of fresh water, pure and limpid at which He can quench His thirst whenever He wishes; but if disquiet enters, then that soul, or rather that water, becomes agitated as though a stick had stirred up the muddy bottom, and then He cannot quench His thirst from it.

Not only that, but the devil delights to fish in troubled waters and finds that state of the soul best adapted to his evil machinations. That is why Jesus forewarned Sister Consolata on September 24th, 1936:

Never let yourself become perturbed, never, never! For when you become perturbed, the devil is content; then his victory will be assured.

This threefold "never" was a confirmation of the obedience which her spiritual director had imposed upon her, for in her great longing for perfection she was inclined somewhat to scrupulosity. Jesus reminded her explicitly:

Remember that you are obliged under obedience never, never, never to let your soul become perturbed! That is for you the most important thing!

We must never lose confidence, therefore, in order never to become troubled. In fact, once we become perturbed, it nearly always follows that we become discouraged; and when we are discouraged, we do not continue to do battle;

therefore we do not advance any more, but are very apt to retreat instead. Nothing is gained, and much is lost. At the very least we lose time. Sister Consolata writes:

"I have come to understand how foolish it would be for a mountain climber to stop his ascent in discouragement if he made a slight slip, and not to dare to look up at the coveted peak any more. On the contrary, if he is wise, he will rise again quickly and will take up his march once more with confidence and undisturbed, firmly determined not to lose any time; at every new slip he will be ready to get to his feet again quickly."

Well intentioned souls will never be able to meditate sufficiently on the following lesson which Jesus taught Sister Consolata on November 7th, 1935:

Tell me, Consolata, which is the more perfect soul: one who is always bewailing to Jesus that she is imperfect, is constantly committing faults, and is unfaithful to her resolutions—or one who is always smiling at Jesus, does what she can to love Him, but does not worry over her involuntary inperfections so as not to lose time; she is intent solely upon continuing to love Jesus. Tell Me which of these souls seems to you to be the more perfect?

"I like the second one better."

Therefore, do what you can to love Me, and when you realize that you have been unfaithful to Me, offer Me a more ardent act of love, and then take up once again your song of love. Jesus is not a tyrant, and if He forgives an entire lifetime of crime in return for one act of love, then tell Me, how could it be that He would take notice one day of some useless thought on which you had dwelt involuntarily? It is a futile lament and a loss of time to keep repeating to Me: 'Look, Jesus, what I have done; how faithless I have been...'

On the contrary, a more ardent act of love enriches your own soul and delights Mine! Do you understand? . . . Do not give a thought to your involuntary imperfections!

We must strive toward perfection, therefore, through loving Jesus; we must make every effort to diminish the number of voluntary faults, but not become discouraged when we happen to commit one: we must always have faith in the immense goodness of the Sacred Heart of Jesus who will not on that account withdraw His love, His favors and His graces from the soul. Jesus gave to all souls, through Sister Consolata, the following invaluable advice:

Believe Me, you will be no less dear to Me even if your weakness permits you to be untrue to your promise of silence, etc. . . . You see, Consolata, My Heart is won more readily through your wretchedness than through your virtues! Who came away from the Temple justified? The publican.[45] *For to Me the sight of a humble and contrite soul is irresistible... That is the way I am.*

Remember always that I love you and will always love you dearly, no matter what fault you may unwillingly commit. Therefore, never, never, never harbor the least doubt that I might not carry out My promises because of some infidelity of yours; never! You would be wounding My Heart deeply if you did, Consolata! Remember that only Jesus can fully understand your weakness; only He knows human frailty in its entirety. Consolata, you must never, never, never commit that fault of doubting that I would keep My promises because of your unfaithfulness! Promise Me that, won't you? Do not offer Me that insult, for you would cause Me great suffering!

---

45. See Luke 18:10.

One must not think that all this applies only to souls in an advanced state of perfection such as Sister Consolata's, who would prefer death to committing an act of unfaithfulness with open eyes. Again we repeat, Jesus intended to speak to all souls through Sister Consolata, and to those also who, at the outset of their spiritual renewal, are feeling the bitterness of the struggle. Saint Francis de Sales once wrote: "The soul who rises from sin to devotion can be compared to the rising sun which does not dispel the darkness in an instant but little by little. A gradual return to health is always more lasting. Diseases of the soul, like those of the body, arrive at a gallop, but depart slowly, step by step."[46]

Jesus was also addressing those who, after having made some progress in the way of perfection and thinking themselves invulnerable, still have to experience what human frailty is when, with God's permission, the enemy attacks unexpectedly and with added violence. As Saint Francis de Sales puts it: "Solomon says that a maid-servant who of a sudden becomes the mistress is a very insolent creature. There is great danger that a soul who has for a long time been a slave to her passions would become proud and conceited if she became mistress over her passions all at once."[47] That is the right moment for gathering all the forces of the soul into one supreme act of confidence in the Sacred Heart of Jesus. Such souls should consider well the following comforting words which Jesus addressed to Sister Consolata on the same occasion as above:

Look, Consolata, the enemy will make every effort to shake your blind faith in Me, but you must never forget that

---

46. *Introduction to the Devout Life,* chapter 5.
47. *Letter to a Lady,* Coll. Blaise, 825.0.

I am, and love to be, exclusively kind and merciful. Understand My Heart, Consolata; understand My love, and never permit the enemy to gain entrance into your soul, even for an instant, with a thought of diffidence; never! Believe Me, I am solely and always kind; I am solely and always like a parent to you![48] *Imitate therefore the children who, at every little scratch of the finger, run at once to mother to have it bandaged. You should always do the same, and remember that I will always cancel out and repair your imperfections and infidelities, just as the mother will always bandage the child's finger, whether it is really hurt or only seems so in imagination. And if the child were to really hurt his arm or his head, how tenderly and affectionately would he be cared for and bandaged by the mother! Well, I do the very same with regard to your soul when you fall, even though I may do it in silence. Do you understand, Consolata? Therefore, never, never, never have even a shadow of doubt! Lack of confidence wounds My Heart to the quick and makes Me suffer!*

Our Lord promised Sister Consolata, however, to her comfort, that He would never permit her to fall into any grave fault:

No, my dear, I will not let you break your arm or your head! But then you must also know that what I am now saying to you, will one day be of use to other souls. That is why I wish you to write it all down.

This divine lesson, then, is intended for all souls, for here on earth no one can pretend to be exempt from defects and imperfections: "If we say we have no sin, we deceive

---

48. See Mark 9:22. Faith in God springs from a lively and practical faith in His power, goodness, and faithfulness.

ourselves, and the truth is not in us."[49] Sister Consolata had her defects, we repeat; nor did she try to conceal them, but rather took delight in exposing them. Hers were mostly external faults as when, in her zeal for the observance of the rule, a sudden utterance escaped her. But how weighty could such faults be in the eyes of God when they happened to one with so ardent a temperament, with so quick and impetuous a character that she was nicknamed "Thunder and Lightning?" Her soul had likely struggled heroically earlier in the day to repress some ten or twenty times the disordered impulses of her nature; and after every unpremeditated utterance she had immediately repented and humbled herself before God and His creatures with a sincere resolve to amend.

In addition, it must also be noted that frequently such defects are a veil used by God to conceal His gifts and workings in a soul from the eyes of others. Saint Juliana of Norwich writes: "In order to lead them to His bliss, God lays on those whom He loves something that is not blameworthy in His own sight, but for which the world will criticize and blame them."[50] That was also the case with Sister Consolata, for in accordance with her explicit request that she might remain inconspicuous in her community, Jesus promised her:

Yes, I will load you with sorrows and humiliations!

What were these humiliations? Precisely that she appeared to have faults, not only in the eyes of others, but even in her own, for in that consists true humiliation. Jesus once responded to a certain soul to whose prayers Saint Gertrude had commended herself in order to overcome some failings:

---

49. I John 1:8.
50. *Revelations of Divine Love*, chapter 28.

Those defects are very advantageous to her. Each day I heap upon her soul such an abundance of graces that, to preserve her human frailty from the assaults of vanity, I must conceal some of them from her own eyes under the cloud of these slight failings.[51]

These are all facts which are well known, but which are forgotten in practice. We forget them in our own regard, and become restless, disturbed, and discouraged when we happen to commit some fault; but above all, we forget them in regard to our neighbor and deny any possible sanctity in a soul if we perceive a shadow of a fault in her.

It should also be added that such defects are more readily found in generous, ardent, and active souls who are aflame with a desire for sanctity, rather than in souls who measure and study each step for fear of stumbling. The saints were not timorous or meticulous, but audacious performers; we do not call them presumptuous but audacious; they did not lose themselves in futile discussions, but aimed at the essential part. "Those who never give battle," says Saint John Chrysostom, "never suffer a wound; it is the ones who throw themselves with ardor at the enemy who often get wounded."[52]

* * *

This digression was necessary, for it is most important that souls and directors of souls should not overlook the essential for the sake of the accessory detail. Note how Jesus continued His parental exhortation and encouraged Sister Consolata:

---
51. P. Cros, S.J., *The Heart of St. Gertrude.*
52. Ad Theod. laps. I, 1.

You would like to have Me promise that I would never permit you to fall but always to remain faithful, always perfect? No, Consolata, I do not wish to deceive you, and therefore I tell you: you will commit faults, infidelities, and imperfections; and these will help you to advance, for they will cause you to make many acts of humility.

Saint Francis de Sales writes: "Oh blessed imperfections which cause us to know our own weakness, and which help us to practice humility, self-contempt, patience, and diligence!"[53]

But while it is easy for a soul to maintain confidence when she is enjoying divine favors, the same cannot be said when the soul is walking in spiritual darkness. In order to prepare Sister Consolata also for that danger, Jesus therefore forewarned her in these words on November 27th, 1935:

Yes, Consolata, to-day the skies of your soul are serene like the skies in nature, rosy and blue. But in a little while this beautiful sky of love and confidence will be blacked out by a profound darkness... Have courage, Consolata! Those will be the fruitful days of trial in which you will be able to show God with deeds what love and confidence you have in Him! Have faith, always have faith in Jesus! If you only knew how much that pleases Me! Give Me always that solace of trusting in Me, even in the darkness of death. Give Me always the joy of hearing you say: 'Jesus, I place my trust in Thee!' no matter in what hour of darkness you may find yourself.

Sister Consolata did just that. She maintained her confidence unaltered, and even increased it. On August 14th, 1934, the Vigil of the Assumption of the Blessed Virgin, she

---

53. Coll. Blaise, Letter 881.

placed in the hands of her heavenly Mother the following vow of confidence:

"My Mother, into your hands I place my vow which I now offer to the Good God, that I will always trust in His goodness, His mercy, no matter in what state my soul may find herself, and will always believe in what He has promised me. Oh my dear Mother, with your assistance I wish to expect, to trust in, and to believe all this from the omnipotence of the Good God. Oh my God, I love Thee, and place my trust in Thee!"

The words "My God, I trust in Thee" or else "Jesus, I trust in Thee" recur continually in the writings of Sister Consolata; they are like a seal to her every intention, every renewal after some fault, every new effort toward perfection. Is it to be marveled at, then, that the Sacred Heart of Jesus let Itself be conquered by such great trust? The divine gifts, the magnificent promises which Christ made to her, are all the fruit and reward of her loving confidence. She believed, and she did so with a faith which not only carried away, or rather destroyed, the mountains of her own faults, but placed the very omnipotence of God at the service of the creature. This Jesus confirmed to her:

(August 6th, 1935) *Do you know what draws Me to your soul? It is the blind faith which you have in Me!*

(October 20th, 1935) *The blind, childlike, limitless faith which you have in Me, pleases Me greatly, and it is on that account that I bend down to you with so much love and with such tenderness.*

Because of that confidence He will work in her marvel upon marvel:

(October 8th, 1935) *I will work wonders in you, Consolata, because your trust in Me has no obstacles. You be-*

lieve in Jesus and in His merciful Heart. *Everything is possible to him who believes!*[54]

Because of that confidence He will bring her to the height of sanctity:

(November 18th, 1935) *If you had trusted in yourself, or had leaned exclusively on one of My creatures in order to gain the summit, you would have advanced at a snail's pace; but since you trust only in Jesus, you are sustained by the Almighty, and so I will work marvels; We will make gigantic flights!*

Because of this trust He will pour the treasures of His divine Heart into her soul:

Consolata, place no limits on your confidence in Me, then I will place no limits on My graces for you!

And because of her confidence He will make of her not only a world apostle but an apostle of apostles. That promise was first made to her on October 22nd, 1935:

Consolata, I will make you an apostle of apostles!

On December 10th, 1935, He confirmed this and explained to her:

God has deigned to take a child and make of her an apostle of the confidence which one should have in God; He will also know how to instill into that child such fortitude as to enable her to withstand all trials and bring her victorious to the longed-for goal.

On November 3rd, 1935, He reassured her concerning the trials which awaited her:

Fear nothing, Consolata! No one can now stop your speedy flight toward the goal, no one; for I am with you,

---

54. See Mark 9:22.

and you must trust solely and blindly and completely in your Jesus. I rejoice in that, and you will see what I will be able to make of Consolata! Fear nothing and no one! God is with you! He is thinking for you, and protects you like the pupil of His eye. I promise that you will fully live up to the designs which Jesus has concerning you. 'He that believeth in Me, out of his belly shall flow rivers of living water.'[55] Do trust in Jesus! Trust always in Jesus! If you only knew how much pleasure that gives Me! Grant Me this solace to trust in Me even in the shadow of death. Never have fear of anything! Trust solely, completely, and always in Jesus! And when darkness envelops your soul, then repeat with even greater ardor: 'Jesus, I behold Thee no longer, I hear Thee no longer, but all my trust is placed in Thee!' Thus you must act in every trial! Your trust in Me is already great, Consolata; in the days of trial let it become heroic!

Heroic it really was! For the spiritual exercises of 1942, when she was already ascending her Calvary, she confided these notes to her diary which merit being reproduced in their entirety:

". . . My soul, can you declare this day in the sight of God that you have always battled, that you have attained the desired perfection, and that you have kept faith with your resolutions? . . . My God, what confusion, what cowardice! . . . But my Jesus, I do not wish to become discouraged! From this moment on I wish to rise, with Thy help, to do battle, to persevere in the fight, so that on the point of death I too may be able to say like Saint Paul: 'I have fought a good fight, I have finished my course, I have kept the faith!'[56]

---

55. John 7:38.
56. 2 Timothy 4:7.

"I know that a continuous, heated, tenacious, and daily struggle awaits me from morning till night, a struggle with my thoughts to keep my mind, my tongue, and my heart pure. I know that it requires a supreme effort of all my energies to offer Thee an unceasing act of love, to see Thee in everything, and to have a generous 'yes' ready for every request; and I also know that Satan's hate will seize every opportunity to hinder or stop me in my loving ascent toward Thee.

"Therefore, the decisive battle is joined against myself, the creature, the enemy. O Jesus, I do not desire to enter heaven one minute sooner than determined by Thee, nor one minute later through some fault of my own. If Thou art for me, who can be against me?[57]

"My Jesus, I desire that from this moment until my death no thought of discouragement or diffidence should arise within me. O Jesus, I wish to begin an act of love as soon as I awake and to continue it in spite of all enemy attacks until I fall asleep at night. O Jesus, always with Thy help, I desire to see Thee, to converse with Thee, to serve Thee in everything! My Jesus, I wish to reply with a 'yes' to Thy every direct or indirect command, every sacrifice, every act of charity, and to accomplish everything with love and with a smile. O Jesus, I wish to live the present moment in an act of love and total dedication to Thy divine will, for Thee and for souls! My Jesus, with the aid of Thy grace I wish to remain at peace and to smile always, no matter what the state of my soul!

"O Jesus, with Thy help I will never turn back! So, since I must advance, why should I do no more than drag

---

57. See Romans 8:31.

myself along? Why should I give the enemy cause to rejoice by my halts and delays, my discouragement and diffidence? . . . No, never again! With Thy aid I desire to go forward, ever forward! Even if wounded, ever forward! And when I shall fall along the way, I wish, with Thy help, to rise again immediately, even if it be the thousandth time and the last moment of the day, and then to take up once more my canticle as though nothing had happened. My good Jesus, bless and preserve that will within me!"

What great good will, what generosity, and what confidence shine forth in this soul! Through the inner conviction of her own nothingness, and through the daily experiencing of her own weakness, she relied solely upon these divine realities: the love, the omnipotence, and the faithfulness of the Sacred Heart of Jesus. She writes:

"One morning during a retreat, I believe it was during the summer of 1931, I had been unable to make my visit to Jesus in the Blessed Sacrament in company with the other novices, and so I knelt down alone before the tabernacle. Upon opening the retreat book I read: 'I believe in Thine omnipotence!' That saying struck me. I closed the book, and then received full divine enlightenment. Divine omnipotence! I came to understand that in spite of all my utter failures and needs, God could still make a saint out of me. I sensed a new and strong hope: confidence in God! If He was omnipotent, if He was able to do anything, He could also fulfill my immense desires! And from that moment I firmly believed that everything would come true. O Jesus, if Thy creature can, with a resolute will, say to Thee this evening: 'I am ready for everything!' to whom do I owe it if not to the merciful Omnipotence who has brought about this miraculous transformation and has substituted His divine strength for my innate weakness!"

Just what were these immense desires of which she speaks, and what divine promises were involved? It appears that she reached the height of her confidence by maintaining ever burning in her heart, and in spite of everything, her faith in the eventual fulfillment of her limitless longings for love, for suffering and for souls, and the corresponding divine promises. Let us quote here from one of her letters to her spiritual director, dated September 10th, 1942:

". . . My most ardent prayer now is to be able to love Jesus as no one has ever loved Him, and to save souls for Him in equal measure. I repeat it to Him at every station of the Cross, even to boring Him. What else can I do, Father? My only hope for obtaining this lies in my insistent prayers. I know I am nothing but wretchedness, inconstancy, and vileness, but I also know that He is omnipotent, that nothing is impossible to Him; therefore, a bridge of confidence is thrown between this little soul and the Good God, and even in my utter worthlessness I believe that Jesus will grant me what I desire.

"No more do I fear sorrows, struggles, destruction. Jesus gives me the grace to love Him; so I would be astonished and saddened if I did not find myself in that state. With great audacity I am asking to suffer as no one has ever suffered, for I do not rely upon myself; vile by nature, I count exclusively on Him, the Omnipotent, who can do everything, even to granting me to bear so much sorrow with joy. I ask for it; I long for it; and I believe that it will be granted to me. Sometimes, jokingly, I tell Him that if He does not grant me suffering and the strength to endure it, He is not omnipotent: 'But I do believe that Thou are omnipotent!' It seems to me,

Father, that I have already started on the road to suffering and love.

"Sometimes in the evening, when I am making the Way of the Cross, I look up at the stars and think of what the saints may be saying about my insistent prayer for so high a degree of love, for suffering, and for souls. . . If only it came from an innocent and faithful heart, but from Consolata! . . . However, the challenge has now been offered by an audacious confidence which hopes to obtain all. To him who believes, everything is possible! And Consolata does believe! O Father, faith seems to have grown so great in me, so great! . . . I cling tenaciously to prayer to keep it so, and if possible to increase it still further. I repeat that the bridge has been thrown across from this maiden to the Heart of God: limitless confidence!"

This enthusiastic and loving confidence explains the promise which Jesus made so many times to that dear soul:

Consolata, within the bosom of the Church, you will be Confidence.

If we may anticipate a little what will be revealed in the coming pages, it is possible to draw this conclusion now, that it is love, the life of love, which really carries the soul to the point of heroism in all virtues, and victoriously overcomes every weakness of human nature.

BE IN LOVE WITH LOVE

The other truth of which the soul must be thoroughly convinced if she desires to make progress in the life of love, is that Jesus asks nothing from us, His poor creatures, but love.

In the same way that all relations between Creator and creature can be summed up in the words of Saint Paul, "He loved me,"[58] just so is this relationship between Creator and creature expressed in this other passage from the Gospel: "Thou shalt love the Lord thy God."[59] Love for love! The most that a creature can give Him is already His, and He can ask for it back, even to life itself. But not so with love; here on earth the creature is free to refuse it. But God desires it, asks for it, claims it; that was the purpose of the creation of man. As Saint Thomas puts it: "The love of God is the end of all human activities and affection."[60] God has proclaimed it as the first commandment, from the observance of which depends the attainment of eternal life.[61] He demands all of it. He wishes to be loved with all the heart, with the whole soul, with the whole mind, and with all one's strength. And in order to gain this our love, He came down from heaven and made Himself man. Not even that sufficed, but He made Himself a beggar at the feet of His creature: "Give Me to drink."[62] And in the end He ascended the gibbet and with the voice of His Blood proclaimed the same divine longing: "I thirst!"[63]

This divine call has remained alive throughout twenty centuries in the voice of the Gospel; then it made itself more urgent through the revelations of Saint Margaret Mary Alacoque; and in these latter times it has been intensified by means of numerous merciful manifestations such as the one which centers around the life and teaching of the Little

---

58. Galatians 2:20.
59. Matthew 22:37.
60. II, II, 27, 6.
61. Matthew 12.
62. John 4:7.
63. John 19:28.

Flower. And yet, how many souls who sincerely desire to reach God are still wandering, restless and famished, over difficult paths, while the direct, easy and secure road lies in front of them: love! Many are ardently longing to consecrate themselves to God, but are held back by some fear of who knows what austerity, as though the divine Bridegroom were thirsting more for our blood than for our love!

Not so! From Sister Consolata Jesus asked only love, although she belonged to one of the most severely cloistered orders; love would then do all the rest. The expressions "love Me only," "love Me always," "love Me deeply," "from you I ask only love," are found repeated hundreds of times in the pages of her diary which carry the divine instructions. It is a continual, insistent, and touching invitation by the Creator who thirsts for the love of His creature. He does not find it among the greater part of mankind, nor does He even receive it in its entirety from many of the souls who are consecrated to Him; so He goes begging for it from the little souls who better understand the longings of the Sacred Heart of Jesus and who respond to it. In fact, Jesus told Sister Consolata on October 15th, 1935:

I long to be loved by innocent hearts, by the hearts of children, by hearts who will give Me all their love!

He is asking for love from souls such as these, so that through them, the entire world might become inflamed with love (October 13th, 1935):

Consolata, love Me on behalf of each and every one of My creatures, of each and every heart that exists. I thirst so much for love!

It is precisely this thirst for love which every human heart ought to feel for its Creator, that the Creator has for the love of His creatures (November 9th, 1935):

Love Me, Consolata! I thirst for your love, just as a parched man thirsts for a spring of fresh water!

So great is this thirst for love that He even said to Sister Consolata on November 3rd, 1935:

Write this down, Consolata—for I demand it of you under obedience—that for one act of love from you I would create heaven!

Even more sublime is what He told her on November 9th, 1935:

Consolata, when you love Me continuously, I enjoy heaven in your heart!

According to the teaching of Holy Scripture, of the Church Fathers, and of theology, every soul who is in a state of grace is truly a temple, a throne, the heaven of God. What then shall one say of a soul who not only lives in love but who lives for love? Jesus told Saint Margaret Mary Alacoque:

My daughter, the desires of your heart please Me so greatly that, if I had not already instituted My divine Sacrament of love, I would institute it for love of you in order to have the pleasure of abiding in your soul![64]

And now, on October 29th, 1935, He tells Sister Consolata:

One of your Communions recompenses Me for all I had to suffer in order to search you out, to find you and to possess you!

"But Jesus, I do not know how to say anything to Thee!"

Never mind; your heart is mine exclusively, and what else do I desire from My poor creatures, but the heart? I do not trouble about anything else. . . Your heart is already Mine for all eternity!

---

64. *Life and Works*, II, 105.

Now we can well understand the divine insistence that Sister Consolata should unite to her unceasing love an unceasing prayer for the coming of the reign of love in the world! Thus, on December 16th, 1935, Jesus told her:

Consolata, when you implore pardon for poor, guilty humanity, then ask for the triumph of My mercy, and implore the burning flame of divine love especially that it may, in a new Pentecost, cleanse humanity from so much sinful filthiness! Oh, only divine love can make apostles out of apostates, immaculate lilies out of soiled ones, and trophies of mercy out of revolting and vicious sinners! Ask from Me love, the triumph of My love over you and over every soul who is now on earth or who will ever exist until the end of time. By means of unceasing prayer, prepare for the triumph of My Heart and of My love throughout the earth!

Another time Jesus reiterated the same idea and quoted the words of the Little Flower: "O Jesus, if only I could relate to all little souls Thine inexpressible affability!" Then He added (November 27th, 1935):

Consolata, tell the little souls, tell everyone, of My ineffable condescension! Tell the world how good I am, how like a parent, and how in return I desire only love from My creatures. You may speak of it, Consolata, and relate My extreme mercy and limitless parental condescension.

Love! That is the fire which Jesus came to bring upon earth and which He desires to enkindle in every human heart (December 15th, 1935):

Oh that I could descend into every heart and pour into it My tender love! . . . Consolata, love Me on behalf of all, and through your prayer and your immolation, prepare the world for the coming of My love!

Jesus, therefore, desires to save the world. But the world must needs turn back to Jesus. With Him there is peace in the tranquility of order, without Him anarchy and ruin. And how does one return to Jesus? There is only one way for souls, as well as for nations: love. That is the whole of the Law, the whole of Christianity. Saint Francis de Sales writes: "Love is the epitome of all theology; it transformed into holy learning the ignorance of a Paul, an Anthony, a Hilarion, a Francis, without the use of books or teachers."[65] Salvation lies in the fulfilling of this one precept which embraces God and neighbor. "This do, and thou shalt live."[66] Protestantism on the one hand and Jansenism on the other have, during these last centuries, extinguished little by little this sacred fire within the heart of Christianity, and have killed it in many souls. The death mask of a Christianity which has been reduced to simple faith or fear has congealed the hearts, has driven them away from God, and has carried them progressively to indifferentism, skepticism, atheism, and paganism.

In order to return to Jesus, it is necessary therefore to return to the Gospel—which Jesus Himself has placed in the bosom of the Catholic Church, and which she has constantly defended and taught: the Gospel of love and of charity.

To believe in the Gospel is to believe in love; to carry the Gospel into practice means to love.

---

65. *Of the Love of God*, Book 8, chapter 1.
66. Luke 10:28.

- III -

THE LIFE OF LOVE AND CHRISTIAN PERFECTION

LOVE IS SANCTITY

GOD alone knows how many holy souls there are within the bosom of the Church Militant; but this much is certain: not a few Christians hold the belief that sanctity is to be found exclusively in the cloister, or at least that sanctity is something reserved for a few privileged souls who receive it like some free gift from heaven which they merely need to accept. Such a way of thinking is not only erroneous but harmful, for it tends to keep souls in a state of spiritual inertia and mediocrity which is not at all befitting to one who professes himself to be a follower of Jesus Christ.

The vocation to sanctity is open to all Christians without distinction, for all are members of one and the same Mystical Body. If the Head is holy, then also the members. When Jesus says in the Gospel: "Be you therefore perfect as also your heavenly Father is perfect,"[1] He is addressing all His followers. When Saint Paul writes: "This is the

---

1. Matthew 5:48.

will of God, your sanctification,"[2] it is again meant for all Christians.

If God desires us to be holy, He will without the slightest doubt also increase the graces needed for us to attain sanctity. All that Jesus has done for us or has given to us, is intended not only for our salvation but for our sanctification. It is precisely the desire, the joy, we might almost say the ambition, of Jesus to see us holy. He confirmed this to Sister Consolata when He said:

If you only knew what joy it gives Me to sanctify a soul! Everybody ought to become holy in order to procure Me this pleasure! Would you like to have a faint idea of it? Then think of the joy which a mother feels when she sees her son return radiant with his well-earned diploma; the happiness of that mother is indescribable! Well, My felicity in seeing a soul attain sanctity, vastly exceeds that faint comparison!

Here again Jesus is speaking of all souls.

It is therefore of the utmost importance that Christians should be well informed on this point. Why should we hesitate to speak about holiness, or why be afraid to aspire to it, if that is the very duty of every Christian? The important thing is to form a correct concept regarding holiness, so as not to go wrong in practice and achieve little or nothing under the impression of achieving much. Nor ought we to shrink from so noble an undertaking on account of our own meanness and weakness.

When speaking of sanctity and saints, it is a mistake to lay stress on the extraordinary and freely given gifts or graces, "gratis datae," and Jesus expressly so declared to Sister Consolata, as we have seen. It is also wrong to stress

---

2. I Thessalonians 4:3.

extraordinary penances, austerities, and the like, as though the first and great commandment of the Law, and hence the first and foremost duty of the Christian, were the mortification of his own body, rather than the love of God and of his neighbor.

No, there is no need to misinterpret the Gospel or to reduce the saints of Christianity almost to the level of a sect of flagellants by not accentuating that inner union with God, that love, from which all works, and especially all virtues, draw life, worth, and perfection. The Gospel is not a message of sadness, but rather one of joy, beginning with the joyous announcement of the angels at Bethlehem and ending with the angels' triumphant words at the empty tomb of Jesus. Who could assert that Our Lord forbids His followers the pure and chaste joys of life which His love has strewn along their path, interwoven with sorrows? And are not the daily sacrifices transfigured in the light of Christian hope? We have already encountered in this message a number of hints in that direction, and we will enumerate still others.

Weakened by a bad case of influenza, Sister Consolata one day supported herself on the choir stall and then even sat down in choir, a thing she never did at other times for the sake of mortification. She regretted it later, however, and asked pardon of Jesus; but He replied:

Be at peace, Consolata, do not make Me out to be a severe Person! Jesus, who sent the raven to awaken your Father Francis belatedly one morning solely because he had had little sleep during the night, can also grant permission to one of His creatures to support herself or sit down in choir because she is suffering from influenza! Do you not understand that Jesus is goodness, mercy, and indulgence itself?

Sister Consolata was very much attached to all regulations of the communal life, also in the matter of food. But she purposely and gladly denied herself those things which the community allowed to its weaker members, and she never wished to vary from that rule of hers, not even when she was physically laid low and infirm. Jesus taught her a beautiful lesson in connection with this point on September 24th, 1936:

Remember, Consolata, that I am kind; do not distort this fact! You see, the world likes to represent sanctity by pictures of austerities, flagellations, chains... But it is not like that. If sacrifice and penance do enter into the life of a saint, they are not on that account the whole of his life. The saint, or the soul who gives herself to Me with generosity, is the most fortunate being on earth, for I am kind, altogether kind.

Never lose sight of the fact that the Jesus whom you behold dying on the Cross at the end of His mortal career, is the same Jesus who for thirty years shared the life which is common to all men, in the bosom of His own family; and He is the same Jesus who all during His three years' ministry sat down to table with men and joined in their banquets. And Jesus was holy, Consolata, the holiest of all men! Therefore, do not misrepresent Me in your need, but remember that Jesus is always kind; to you He is and ever will be parental tenderness itself until the very end of your life.

I do love the fidelity with which you are keeping your promises, but I also love your confidence in My parental goodness, and it will please Me if you will make exceptions when there is a real need for it. Remember, and never forget: Jesus is kind! Do not misrepresent Me!

So it is not really a case of omitting something which might serve to sanctify the soul; but everything has its proper place, and everything has its proper value in the order of self-sanctification. In short, if in the Gospel Jesus calls all His followers to sanctity and gives them all an example of it, then there can of necessity be only one single sanctity for all, and it must be attainable by all. There are divers ways leading to it, however, according to the diverse conditions of people and the varying designs which God has for souls.

Sanctity consists essentially in love, for that is what unites the soul to the fountain of all sanctity, Jesus Christ. While He does not require the same sacrifices in the same measure from all, He does desire to be loved by all; and not only that, but to be loved with all the heart, with all the mind, with one's whole soul, and with one's whole strength. He requires this total love from everyone by a definite commandment which is the very essence of the entire Law. Therefore, when a soul gives Him this all, she is holy; and she is holy in the measure in which she loves Him to the exclusion of all else; and this, as we shall see, she can only achieve by renouncing everything which is opposed to perfect love.[3]

Jesus taught Sister Consolata on December 16th, 1935:

Tell all souls, Consolata, that I prefer an act of love and a Communion of love to any other gift which they may offer Me! Yes, an act of love is better than the discipline, for I thirst for love. Poor souls! They think that in order to reach Me it is necessary to live an austere, penitential life! . . . See how they misrepresent Me. They make Me out as one to be feared, whereas I am kindness itself! See how they forget the precept which I have given them, the very essence of

---

3. Luke 14:33.

the entire Law: 'Thou shalt love the Lord thy God with thy whole heart, with thy whole soul. . .'

To-day, as yesterday and tomorrow, I ask only and always for love from My poor creatures!

Ah, if Christians would only understand more deeply the spirit of the Gospel, how much more easily and happily they would put it into practice in their daily lives! Love in return for love, that is everything!

INTIMATE LIFE OF LOVE WITH JESUS

The scope and fruit of a life of love is, therefore, the union of the soul with Jesus for the attainment of sanctity. This is the treasure of which the Gospel speaks that the man discovered; for its sake he sold all his possessions and bought the field in which it was hidden. That auspicious field is equanimity, and to gain it one must divest oneself of everything by a rigorous mortification of the heart and of the senses, both internal and external.

Not everyone can understand this language; in fact there are relatively few souls even among the dedicated ones who succeed in discovering this treasure. Or, if they have caught a glimpse of it, they do not come into possession of it because they will not impose upon themselves the necessary renunciation. They could be leading a divine and divinely fruitful life, but instead they stop short at the threshold of the King's palace and settle down to a way of life which is little more than mediocre, or at least is far removed from that perfection to which they are consecrated.

Jesus, the King of Love, gives all, but He also demands

all: every heartbeat, every thought of the mind, every reaction of the senses, and every capacity of the soul. Then He places no limits on His gifts or on His giving of Himself; the soul is as it were absorbed into Him and lives and works in Him in so ineffable an intimacy of affections and intentions as is found only among the citizens of heaven.

Every request for love which Our Lord made to Sister Consolata aimed precisely at this: to bring her to an actual, living, intimate, and stable union with Himself. It is not surprising, therefore, that in His instructions He demanded ever more and in the end permitted her no voluntary distractions.

Do not turn your glance away from Jesus for any reason whatsoever; then you will reach the eternal shores more rapidly! (August 8th, 1935)

He desired to see her perfect in everything, but especially so on this point from which the virtues derive their perfection:

I desire you to be perfect! I want you continually with Me! Therefore, Jesus only! I alone suffice for everything. You trust Me, do you not? (October 10th, 1935)

He did not segregate her physically from other creatures. On the contrary, He always demanded from her a perfect community life in everything, including recreation; nevertheless, she had to see to it that always and everywhere her mind and her heart were not distracted from Jesus:

Do you know what I desire from you? Continuous intimacy, without even an instant's distraction; always united with Me, even when you must converse with creatures. (August 5th, 1936)

One day she left the door to her cell open in order to

have a little more air, and so she was observed at her work. Jesus told her:

Consolata, close the door of your cell to every earthly sound, and leave only the window open to all that is heavenly.

A similar exhortation was given her about the door of the senses which is more dangerous and distracting:

Just as you close the door of your cell (for solitude is so beautiful), so you must also close every door to the senses. Let us always live in intimacy, you and I alone. Close the entrance to every thought, to everything. Just the two of us alone, always! (October 29th, 1935)

Thus intimately united to the Saint of Saints, the soul will advance on the road to sanctity with sure and rapid strides. Of course she will still have to force herself to respond always to the actions of grace and particularly to be faithful to her resolutions which actually make grace operative. This is what Jesus told Sister Consolata on June 23rd, 1935:

I am always faithful to My promises! If you remain always in Me, you too will remain faithful to what you have promised and resolved, for what is found in the vine is also found in the branch.

Not only does Jesus grant the soul fidelity to her resolutions, but He pours into it all the virtues which in Him are found in an infinite measure, and He does so in proportion as the soul is united with Him:

If you are in Me and we are one, then you will bring forth much fruit and will become strong, for you will disappear like a drop of water in the ocean; My silence will pass into you, and My humility, My purity, My charity, My gen-

tleness, My patience, My thirst for suffering, and My zeal for souls whom I wish to save at all costs! (August 22nd 1935)

A perfect union of hearts will always bring with it a sharing of goods, and so in our case, since the soul possesses nothing of her own, the possessions of Jesus will become hers. Many were the times that Jesus repeated to Sister Consolata, while exhorting her to that intimate union with Himself: *All that is Mine is yours, Consolata!* (not only all virtues but) *all My words, My thoughts, and therefore also My suffering and My love!*

This is the superabundant fruit of sanctification, and it is also that of the apostolate; these two gifts, sanctity and souls, are inseparable and stand in direct relation to one another:

Since you are longing to love Me and to save souls for Me, dwell in Me always, at work and during recreation... Do not leave Me for an instant! Then you will bear much fruit. Look at Saint Peter. He had been fishing all night long and had caught nothing; but together with Me, he pulled in his nets filled with fish almost as soon as he had cast them into the water.

It will be the same with you if you never leave Me for an instant. Whenever you receive from Me an inspiration to mortify yourself, throw out your net in response, and you will haul it in filled with souls—souls whom you will not know until you reach heaven. (November 19th, 1934)

These lessons are of value to both cloistered and uncloistered souls, for sanctity is the foundation of the apostolate, just as union with Jesus is the foundation for sanctity; and it is precisely love which brings about such a union. Jesus once made this comment on the words of Saint John:

God is charity; and he that abideth in charity, abideth in God, and God in him.[4] *You see, I am Love, and as long as you remain in Love, you remain in Me and I also in you. Therefore, even when I am silent and when you no longer hear My voice, remember always that as long as you love Me, I am in you and you in Me! . . . Is it not true that you desire to love Me alone and always? Therefore, I remain always in you and you in Me!*

So, if love is the means by which we attain union with Jesus, it follows that, the more perfect our love is, the more perfect will also be our union with Him.

FERVOR OF LOVE IN PURITY OF SPIRIT

In practice, such perfect love, and therefore such perfect union with Jesus, cannot be attained except through a threefold virginal purity, that of mind, of speech, and of heart. Jesus indicated this when He told Sister Consolata on April 19th, 1936:

When you are praying you feel the need of being enveloped in silence; and so too, in order to be united with Me, it is necessary that a profound silence should reign in your innermost being. Any little noise disturbs prayer; in a similar way, any mere trifle that distracts you, disturbs your fervor. Immaculateness is always required!

This immaculate purity seems to correspond to what Saint Thomas teaches: "From men's affections must be excluded not only that which is contrary to charity, but also

---

4. I John 4:16.

all that which might be a hindrance to giving oneself entirely to God."[5]

According to the divine teaching, this virginal purity comprises a threefold silence: that of the thoughts (purity of mind), that of words (purity of speech), and that of interests (purity of heart). From this it can be seen that the life of love, if practiced in all its perfection, is anything but a playing with words; no one can make any progress in it who is not determined to sacrifice everything else for it; no great austerities are needed, but rather a mystical crucifixion of all the senses.

First, as regards the purity of mind through a silence of thoughts: "Thou shalt love the Lord thy God with thy whole heart, . . . and with thy whole mind."[6] This is not some advice given to Religious, but a command addressed to all Christians; in fact it is the first of the commandments. Therefore, it must be carried out. God does not command the impossible, and so it must be possible to carry it out, but of course in a varying measure according to each one's state and the grace of God. In any case an effort is required. In this respect also Jesus demanded the highest perfection from Sister Consolata:

Consolata, you know that I love you very much! My Heart is divine, yes, but it is also human like yours; and so it longs for your love, for your every thought. . . I shall take care of everything, even the most trivial matters, but you must think only of Me! I long for your love! So have no other thoughts; they would be like thorns in My Head! (March 24th, 1934)

---

5. II, II, 184, 2.
6. Matthew 22:37.

"This jealousy which God feels toward us," writes Saint Francis de Sales, "is one of supreme friendship, for it is not His concern but our own that we should love Him."[7]

Useless thoughts which are voluntarily admitted by the soul, are thorns in the Head of Jesus, but it requires a bitter struggle for the soul to renounce such thoughts and calls for innumerable acts of self-denial. The thorns which the soul wishes to spare Jesus, must be inflicted upon herself, upon her own head:

Behold Jesus crowned with thorns! You can imitate Him in a very real manner by not permitting one other thought, nothing else to enter your mind. In that way souls will be brought to salvation, and you yourself will be free to love. (August 2nd, 1935)

This is not a passing crown of thorns but a lifelong one, if the soul desires to maintain her purity of mind:

From the moment that the Crown of Thorns first circled My Head, I have never laid it down again. You must do the same; your one thought must be to love. And do you know when you do remove your crown of thorns? When you linger over some useless thought!

This struggle against useless thoughts is certainly among the most difficult, as Sister Consolata experienced throughout her whole life. But the battle has to be conducted with proper tactics, with calmness and gentleness, with great patience and even greater constancy, and without pretending that one's purity of mind could ever achieve a perfection which is not of this life.

"You ask," writes Saint Francis de Sales, "how you might go about concentrating your spirit completely on God

---

7. *Of the Love of God*, Book 10, chapter 13.

so that nothing could pull it back or detach it. To do that, two things are necessary: to die and to be saved. For then there will be no more separation. . ."⁸

In fact it does not depend upon the soul whether she is more or less assailed by useless thoughts. No soul, no matter how perfect, can pretend to become free from this struggle; she would be deluding herself if she believed it would ever come to an end. It suffices for the soul not to admit such useless thoughts voluntarily, as Jesus explained to Sister Consolata:

You see, Consolata, thoughts which come to you without your desiring them, do not make for unfaithfulness. (October 5th, 1935)

This struggle even forms a part of the divine plan for the sanctification of the soul:

I leave you the struggle against useless thoughts, for it is meritorious for you. (October 13th, 1935)

The more insistent the battle, the greater the merit for the soul:

Do you desire the useless thoughts? No. Then everything is to your merit. When one desires only to love, then everything that obstructs that love becomes meritorious. Do you understand? (October 31st, 1935)

Not only is this meritorious for one's own soul, but it is also profitable for other souls:

I permit this assailing battle of thoughts which oppresses you, because it glorifies Me and gives Me souls. Offer Me these undesired thoughts at every instant with this ejaculation: 'For Thee and for souls!' I will transform these thoughts which come to you from morning to night, and which hinder

---

8. Treatise IX on *Modesty.*

your love, into graces and blessings for souls. (October 20th, 1935)

In this also, therefore, Jesus is content with the effort made by His poor creatures. The effort is necessary, however, for it is impossible to love God with one's whole mind unless the mind be immaculately free from other thoughts.

✧   ✧   ✧

Together with purity of mind, Jesus demanded from Sister Consolata also virginal purity of speech, for without this the former would be almost impossible. Every useless word always causes a slight dissipation of the spirit, and this destroys intimacy with Jesus. All souls who have led an interior life have loved silence. So also Saint Teresa, the Little Flower, of whom Father Petitot writes: "She is determined never to transgress the law of silence. This silence which was and ever will be one of the foundations of the ascetical life, is understood by Saint Teresa of the Child Jesus as perfectly and in all its sovereign efficacy as it would be by one who is founding a religious order. As a result, she shows an astounding respect for religious silence; she dedicates to it a veritable cult."[9] It may be claimed that all this applies only to cloistered souls. But even though the exigencies may vary for different souls, it is nevertheless true that Jesus has told all His followers: "I say unto you, that every idle word that men shall speak, they shall render an account for it in the day of judgment."[10]

It should not cause wonderment, therefore, that Jesus demanded from Sister Consolata not only all her thoughts but also all her words:

---

9. P. H. Petitot, O.P. *Una Rinascita Spirituale,* e. I.–IV.
10. Matthew 12:36.

Now that all your thoughts are Mine,[11] give Me also all your words; I desire them all. I desire a continuous silence. I wish you to belong entirely to Me. Have no fear, I will take the responsibility for your thoughts and for your words as well; that is, I will see to it that you will be able to keep these two promises. Are you content? Will you trust Me? (March 30th, 1934)

This silence which Jesus demanded from her included, besides that required by the rule, also a determination not to speak unless she was spoken to, except of course as might be required out of charity:

I wish you to think of Me alone and not to speak unless you are questioned. Then I will always give the answer, and you must not be astonished at the replies which will be pronounced by you, for it is I who will be giving them. (July 14th, 1935)

This and the following rules about silence are not intended for every soul who has been called to follow Sister Consolata, and in particular not those rules which refer to the time of recreation. From Sister Consolata Jesus demanded such a rigorous silence not only from certain motives which we will explain immediately, but above all because He wished to bring her to the utmost perfection in the continuity and purity of her love. On the other hand it is also certain that, without some vigorous and constant effort at eliminating useless thoughts and words, it is impossible to achieve true fervor in loving Jesus.

---

11. To be understood in the sense that she had made Him a gift of them by a formal promise.

Sister Consolata had to limit herself to what was strictly required even when necessity or charity compelled her to speak:

Keep silence always. Be miserly even with necessary words. Instead, give everyone a smile in exchange, and always keep a smiling countenance. (August 2nd, 1935)

Concerning silence during her various activities of the day, Jesus suggested to her:

When you are in doubt as to the choice of one of two activities, then always choose the one in which you will be more by yourself, where you will be better able to keep silence, and so will be better able to love. That is My wish. (August 22nd, 1936)

The Capuchin nuns have about a half hour of recreation each day. Sister Consolata took a regular part in this community activity, and the norm which Jesus gave her to follow was this:

During recreation speak only when the conversation tends to become harmful, and then change the subject.

Outside of such cases, she was to keep to her resolution not to speak unless questioned, even during recreation time.

This applied not only to ordinary days but also to great solemnities when the Capuchin rule of silence was dispensed with:

On this day also, when your rule of silence is suspended, have a smile for everyone, but speak with no one unless you are spoken to; otherwise you will only regret it. (December 8th, 1935)

She experienced this regret, as a matter of fact, for on August 16th, 1936, she writes in her diary:

"Jesus makes certain demands, and once He has asked for something, He requires it always; for example, the matter of silence on the days when the rule is suspended. I gave in during these festive days (the Assumption of the Blessed Virgin Mary), and to-night my poor soul is all torn asunder. Our Lord has had compassion and has reminded me that tiny tots are always getting themselves soiled, and still the mother goes on lovingly changing their clothes, brushing their disheveled hair and washing their faces, in short, making the child look proper once more, though she is convinced that it will be so only for a short while. So it is with me: In the morning I am determined to live the heroic life which Jesus desires, but then . . . everything falls to pieces! I start in again with rigorous silence, over and over again."

In the matter of silence, then, Sister Consolata had to struggle continuously. She was of an extreme simplicity and frankness and was altogether incapable of deceit toward herself or others. She always gave expression to what her heart felt and that, among other things, caused her many a humiliation and penance; so much so that one day Jesus Himself had to give her encouragement by saying:

A soul who really belongs to Me and is possessed by Me becomes like oil which steadfastly refuses to become fused with some contrary fluid such as vinegar or water. That is the explanation of your abhorrence of all that is not truth, simplicity, frankness, obedience, and so forth. That is why, during a temptation, if the enemy does succeed in penetrating with some uncharitable thought, he is not able to remain within you, and escapes at the first opportunity. And so, besides giving you an occasion to humiliate yourself, it will also force you to be more vigilant in the future. Such thoughts cannot remain in you, you see, for I wish to dwell in you all alone.

Purity of mind was, therefore, necessary in order to

deny the enemy an entrance through thoughts, impressions, and so forth. And purity of speech was necessary in order to avoid the above failings which do not cease to be such even though they be involuntary. Jesus confirmed this on September 14th, 1935:

Remain firm in your vow never to speak unless spoken to. In that way you will avoid all defects and imprudent acts, and you will be certain that when you do give a reply, your words will always be such as are desired and blessed by Me.

Jesus here points out that Sister Consolata should avoid not only defects but even imprudent acts. She had to exercise great care to keep the divine activities in her soul from being discovered—no easy matter in a religious community where conversation turns mostly on spiritual arguments. One sentence, one word might be enough to betray her! Sister Consolata understood this well, for she wrote to her spiritual director:

". . . You see, Father, it is more than necessary for me never to speak unless spoken to, even during recreation, for it would be dangerous to give expression to my thoughts and feelings. In this as in other small matters I see the Hand of God. Jesus desires me to be really all His, and so during recreation period my cell has a great attraction for me."

Purity of speech, therefore, like purity of thought was not acquired by Sister Consolata at a cheap price or in the twinkling of an eye. It was rather a continuous struggle with herself all through life and required a strenuous effort. Let us quote from some of her writings:

"I desire, I desire, I desire with all my strength not to permit one useless thought to enter, and not to speak unless spoken to."

"Jesus did not deny His heavenly Father one single thought, one single word or action; He gave Him all. I must do the same and give Him truly everything, my every thought, and a perpetual silence."

"The effort made by Jesus at Gethsemane made Him sweat blood. I will not let a useless thought enter at any cost, nor will I utter one sentence more than is strictly necessary."

"Things go better now during recreation, (July 1936) but my nature has not yet been completely downed and still lets me take a ready pleasure in talking. But now, rather than to keep from speaking unless spoken to, I must pay attention to replying only with what is really necessary. How true it is that we women love to talk!"

We could fill pages and pages with similar confessions and resolutions. She was continually renewing her good will, and never letting herself become disarmed by any difficulty or failure. When she was asked during her last illness to leave a parting counsel with her beloved community, she replied:

"Observe the silence! For from my own experience too I know that the greatest number of faults in a religious community come from not observing the prescribed silence."

*   *   *

Purity of mind and of speech is favored by and integrated into purity of heart. Besides imposing upon the religious soul an effective and affective detachment from the things of the outside world, it also requires a detachment from all that constitutes the little interior world of the convent, and above all an absolute ban on every unhealthy interest in the affairs of others. Given her temperament, this was the point over which Sister Consolata had to struggle the hardest. Her shortcomings with respect to purity of mind and speech nearly always resulted from her not having freed herself from other interests. She writes:

". . . The principal obstacle to loving was my tongue, and during my novitiate it was the virtue of silence which I most strove after. But what a multiplicity of falls until I was able to observe it! Resolutions, struggles, and then, at the very moment when I was victorious, a sentence escaped me, and I was greatly perturbed.

"One day during a novena Jesus said to me: *What is it that keeps you from loving Me, Consolata? It is useless thoughts and being interested in others!* I promised not to interest myself in anyone. But after struggling for days, and after telling myself innumerable times: 'That does not interest me, that does not concern me, etc.' at the next occasion that remark which I had so often choked down, escaped me. One evening during meditation Our Lord made me vividly understand the consequences of my defect, so that I wrote down these lines: 'In the divine light I have come to understand that my tongue is bringing me to hell!' Renewed resolutions, renewed falls. My weakness was extreme and formed my humiliation.

"I experienced violent struggles at table. One sentence will explain it all: 'Mother Abbess, from these souls who kill themselves with extraordinary penances, I would require slavish obedience! . . .' But Jesus wished to combat such tendencies within me and said to me one night while I was standing near the window of my cell: *Consolata, if, while you are contemplating the sky, you let your eyes rest on the windows of the neighboring houses, you will find death. Similarly, if, instead of loving Me alone, you rest your eyes on the actions of others, you will find death!' That taught me a lesson!"*

That taught her a lesson, but it did not free her from the struggle. That never happened. Jesus Himself still had to intervene and admonish her more than once in this regard. Thus, during November, 1934:

Follow Me! What do your Sisters matter to you?[12] You must think solely of following Me!

This is not saying that a Religious should not have the good of her Sisters at heart, but rather that she should never desire that good in opposition to the good of her own soul or to the designs of God which are not the same for all souls; she is simply not to become involved in matters which do not concern her. Here, for example, is how Jesus instructed Sister Consolata concerning extraordinary penances which He did not desire from her, but to which certain other Sisters felt themselves drawn:

You see, Consolata, in heaven every choir of angels attends to the fulfillment of its own office without envying or desiring the office of another. Thus, in a community each one must attend to her own mission without envying or longing for something which pertains to another soul. In your community, in choir, and everywhere, you must be my little Seraph, and therefore you must attend solely to loving without envying or desiring the mission of your other Sisters!

On another occasion Jesus desired to cut short any tendency in this direction by saying:

You must, under obedience, pay no attention to what your Sisters give Me! I and you, that suffices! (June 2nd, 1936)

---

12. See John 21:22.

On the evening before He withdrew His sensible presence from her, Jesus requested among other things also this:

Promise Me that you will not interest yourself in Sister X either directly or indirectly. No matter whether she observes the rule or not, whether she follows the community life in all simplicity or takes extraordinary paths with subterfuges, never mind! Promise Me that you will not speak or think of it, just as though she did not exist in the community. Do solely what charity or your tasks demand! (December 1st, 1935)

One day when Sister Consolata was undecided as to whether to speak or keep silent about a certain Sister, Our Lady also gave her to understand:

"Do not trouble yourself about what is happening in other convents; do the same here, and consider yourself a pilgrim and a stranger with just one duty: to love!"

In order to break once and for all with that fiendish interesting of herself in the concerns of others, Sister Consolata's ardent spirit finally had recourse to the same proven means: she bound herself by a vow on May 26th, 1936:

". . . During meditation the enemy labored to distract my thoughts by making me concerned about the problems of others under the pretext of zeal. I found these concerns to be an obstacle across my path and had to free myself once and for all. Grace then inspired me to bind myself by a new vow, to be renewed at every temptation, and that this would help me to be always victorious. I knew intuitively that my spiritual director would approve such a vow, and so I promised: 'I will not concern myself with anything which occurs in the community, nor with anyone.'"

This vow proved extremely helpful, but the struggle against outside interests continued with more or less vehemence until the end of her life and required from her a continuous and heroic effort of the will.

We must also keep in mind that this triple purity of mind, of speech, and of heart, must not be an end in itself but a means for advancing in the perfection of love. Jesus declared this expressly on June 17th, 1934:

Forget everything and everybody, and think only of loving Me more! Concentrate your every thought, every heartbeat, every silence upon this one thing: to love! And on August 18th, 1936:

Do not think of anything, anything, anything else but to love Me and to suffer with all possible love; that is sufficient!

For of what use would it be to deny oneself speech and outside interests if Jesus were not in the heart? It is not a question, therefore, of silence for the sake of silence, but of silence for the sake of love, and of love for the sake of a life of union with Jesus:

Consolata, you will experience Jesus most intensely if you absolutely eliminate every other thought and rigorously repress every word! (November 6th, 1934)

What does it mean to experience Jesus intensely? It means to live so closely united to Him, that one almost ceases to exist and becomes transformed into Him, becomes as it were identified with Him and as if deified in Him. And this is precisely what Saint Paul said of himself: "I live, now not I; but Christ liveth in me."[13] And Jesus told Sister Consolata on November 6th, 1934:

If you will obliterate yourself and will not permit any outside thought to enter, then I will be thinking within you;

---

13. Galatians 2:20.

if you will not speak, then I will speak within you; if you will stop following your own will, then I will act within you; it will no more be you who lives, but I in you.

In this way the soul and all her strength and activity remains as it were divinized, and who can tell what marvelous strides she will then make day by day toward her own sanctification? That is why Jesus said to Sister Consolata on June 23rd, 1935:

Bid farewell for good to every thought, every word; let others do what they will; you must remain in Me! You will gather much fruit, for I will be the one who acts.

Sister Consolata's every effort was aimed at eliminating thoughts, words, and outside interests in order to achieve a fervent love of Jesus. He desired nothing else from her, for in that lies true and complete holiness:

Remember and keep it well fixed in your mind, you who long so much to gather abundant fruit: in the Gospels I did not declare that you would bring forth much fruit if you undertook extraordinary mortifications, but that you would do so if you remained in Me. Therefore, do not depart from the straight road, but devote your every effort to remaining well united with the Vine. Do not separate yourself from the thought of 'Jesus only!' not even by a single thought or an uncalled-for word. I will think of everything!" (September 26th, 1935)

A soul who wishes to make progress in the life of love must keep ever before herself these lessons which Jesus taught to Sister Consolata concerning the purity of spirit. Although it is true that extraordinary means are not for all souls, it is nevertheless true that the perfection of charity in its ordinary way is intended for all souls, even to its complete flowering. Thus it is commanded by the first and great commandment of the Law. Those who affirm that the life of love is reserved for only a few souls, are stating something that is contrary to both the letter and the spirit of the Gospels.

THE LOVING SOUL GIVES ALL TO JESUS

God has insisted many times that the soul must concentrate her efforts on the one duty: to love. This points clearly to the fact that love is everything and that, therefore, by means of love the soul really gives everything to Jesus. Was not this the great discovery which gave wings to the Little Flower and enabled her to achieve her own sanctification and to carry out her magnanimous desire for an apostolate? "It was charity," she writes, "which gave me the key to my vocation. I came to understand that if the Church had a body, made up of various members, she surely would not be lacking the most necessary and most noble of all organs: the Church must also have a heart, and that inflamed with love. I came to understand that it was love alone which made her members act. If love had ever become extinguished, the apostles would not have proclaimed the Gospel and the martyrs would have refused to shed their blood. I also understood that love embraces all vocations, that love is everything."[14]

As far as the Little Flower's soul was concerned, this was for her a discovery. But this could not be said regarding the Catholic Church's doctrine. When well considered, the above words of the saint are really only an echo of the

---

14. *The Story of a Soul,* chapter 11.

teaching of the great Apostle. He reminds us first of the sublime truth of our incorporation in Christ: "You are the body of Christ, and members of member."[15] Therefore, every member has his own proper gift and must not envy the gifts of the others but rather aspire to the highest gifts. He adds: "I show unto you a yet more excellent way."[16] That is, one that is better than all the charismatic gifts, better than any of the offices which can be held in the Church, and better than any of the works which are carried on in the Church. What is this way? In reply the Apostle delivers that marvelous hymn of love which can justly be called the dogmatic and moral synthesis of the Gospel message. It forms the entire 13th chapter of his Epistle to the Corinthians, and we print here its first part, for we will have occasion to refer to it again:

"If I speak with the tongues of men, and of angels, and have not charity, I am become as sounding brass, or a tinkling cymbal. And if I should have prophecy and should know all mysteries, and all knowledge, and if I should have all faith, so that I could remove mountains, and have not charity, I am nothing. And if I should distribute all my goods to feed the poor, and if I should deliver my body to be burned, and have not charity, it profiteth me nothing."

If every good work therefore—learning, faith, alms, sacrifice, and even martyrdom—both individually and as a whole, is as nothing and has no value without love, it follows that only love counts, only love is in truth everything. And so even a soul who has not been called to such works, or for whom it is impossible to carry them out, is really giv-

---

15. I Corinthians 12:27.
16. I Corinthians 12:31.

ing everything to God when she loves Him with all her heart, with all her mind, with all her strength.

This, we repeat, was the point of departure for Saint Teresa when she embraced the path of love, and it was the same with Sister Consolata, to whom Jesus declared:

Love Me, Consolata, love Me alone! Love is everything, and so you will be giving Me everything. (August 7th, 1935)

When you love Me, you give Jesus everything He desires from His creature: love! (September 20th, 1935)

Our Lord did not wish her to dissipate her spiritual energies in a multitude of often inconclusive resolutions, when this one resolve to love would comprise all others:

Love is everything! If you will now concentrate upon this one resolution, you will be giving everything to Jesus! (December 1st, 1935)

There is no doubt about one's having to obey the Law; and who does? The one who loves. "If anyone love Me, he will keep My word."[17] Jesus told Sister Consolata on November 15th, 1935:

You see, Consolata, My creatures make Me out as one who is fear inspiring rather than kind; and I, on the other hand, delight in being always and solely kind. What is it that I require? Love, and love only, for he who loves Me, serves Me.

Conversely, he who does not love is already outside the Law: "He that loveth Me not, keepeth not My words."[18] And he who observes the Law only out of fear, would not be performing a perfect work, as Jesus explained to Sister Consolata on November 16th, 1935:

---

17. John 14:23.
18. John 14:24.

You see, I long to have My creatures serve Me out of love. Therefore, if a soul avoids some fault for fear of My chastisements, that is not what I am longing for from My creatures. I desire to be loved; I crave the love of My creatures! When they will come to love Me, they will no longer offend Me. When two people really love each other, they never offend each other. That is precisely the way it ought to be between the Creator and His creatures.

One day Sister Consolata was deeply impressed by a sentence she had heard during meditation and asked Our Lord:

"O Jesus, is it not true that if one is blameworthy for performing some work negligently, then one is blessed if one performs it diligently?" Jesus replied:

Rather than with diligence you should strive to do everything with much love. Whether you are working, eating, drinking, or sleeping, do everything with a great deal of love, for I thirst for love. Love is what I look for in every work. (November 29th, 1935)[19]

At other times also Jesus insisted on this point of giving value to every action through love:

Fix all your attention upon your task of the moment so as to accomplish it with all possible love. (October 10th, 1935)

Your actions will have more value in proportion as you increase in love! (November 16th, 1935)

The same thing may be said of every difficulty which the soul encounters. How great must have been the value of the roses of Saint Teresa in the eyes of God because of the fervor with which they were gathered and offered! We

---

19. See I Corinthians 10:31.

find the same language and almost the identical expressions used by Jesus in His instructions to Sister Consolata:

Transform everything disagreeable that you meet with into little roses; gather them with love and offer them to Me with love. (November 14, 1935)

I delight in gifts which are offered with all possible love. Then even your trifles become precious to Me. (December 3rd, 1935)

It is not, therefore, the offering itself which Jesus considers, or its kind; for what can we give Him that is not already His? "If I should be hungry, I would not tell thee; for the world is Mine and the fullness thereof."[20] But our love, yes; that is our own, and that is what Jesus looks for. He told Sister Consolata on November 24th, 1935:

No, Consolata, no! Jesus does not demand heroic acts from you, but merely trifles; only they must be offered with all your heart!

All this must be a comfort to those souls—and they form the great majority—who are not called to perform great works but pass all their lives in performing their humble daily duties, unseen and unappreciated by the world. Sister Consolata was arranging a bunch of flowers for Our Lady one morning, but they were already fairly wilted, and she was regretting this. Then the voice of grace gave her to understand:

"It is not always possible to offer God beautiful flowers of virtues, but they can always be accompanied by love. Jesus does not look at the flower but at the love with which it is offered."

The soul is wise, therefore, in aiming directly at love

---

20. Psalm 49:12.

with a determined effort while practicing a virtue, rather than striving for acts of virtue, for it is love which gives life to the virtues and perfects them. If mutual brotherly love "covereth a multitude of sins,"[21] how can one doubt but that love replaces before God the defects to which a soul is subject. Truly, it is either a case of simple physical failings, and these do not count, or of venial ethical shortcomings, and these, as we shall soon see, are first made good by love and then gradually eliminated. A purely formal perfection is directly opposed to that essential perfection which is in the heart. In fact, any virtue which is not related to the ultimate and perfect Good, though still a virtue, is an imperfect one. One can understand, therefore, how Jesus could say to Sister Consolata:

When the heart is very sick, it makes even a robust person inactive. Thus, if the heart does not belong to Me, I do not know what to make of the soul, no matter how much she is adorned with virtues.

To sum up, that soul is more perfect who comes closer to God. And as God is Love, that soul comes nearer to Him and is the more perfect who loves Him the more. Jesus confirmed this to Sister Consolata when He said:

That soul is dearest to Me who loves Me the most!

LOVE RECEIVES ALL FROM JESUS

The soul who loves Jesus with all her heart and all her strength of spirit not only gives all to Jesus, but also receives

---

21. I Peter 4:8.

all from Him, both for her own sanctification and for the salvation of souls. We will limit ourselves here to a consideration of what concerns the sanctification of the soul.

It is the loving soul above all others who feels the need of not toying with ephemeral wishing and empty protestations of love, but of furnishing a proof of her love by giving herself completely. That soul has understood the truth just stated that, in order to be meritorious and fruitful of good for oneself and others, good works must proceed from love, and that it is love itself that suggests them, sustains them, vivifies them, and makes them perfect.

In other words, it is not wrong to cling to good works in order to arrive at love, but it is more logical and we might say more theologically true to cling to love in order to arrive at good works. Saint Francis de Sales gave this reply to one who told him he desired to be very humble so as to be able to love the Lord deeply: "I, however, wish to love the Lord a great deal in order to be very humble." Which of these paths is the right one? We stand with Saint Francis de Sales who in turn agrees with Saint Paul when he wrote: "Charity is patient, is kind; charity envieth not, dealeth not perversely; is not puffed up; is not ambitious, seeketh not her own, is not provoked to anger, thinketh no evil; rejoiceth not in iniquity, but rejoiceth with the truth; beareth all things, believeth all things, hopeth all things, endureth all things."[22]

Saint Francis de Sales writes further: "Saint Paul does not merely say that charity produces patience, meekness and the like, but he states that charity itself is patient, meek, etc. . . . It is in fact a characteristic of the higher virtues . . .

---

22. I Corinthians 13:4-7.

that they cannot only cause the lesser virtues to become operative, but that they themselves can also fulfill what they demand of the others. . . Hence Saint Thomas writes concerning this assertion of Saint Paul's: 'Charity brings all works of virtue to perfection.'[23] And Saint Ambrose, writing to Demetrius, calls patience and these other virtues 'members of charity.' Saint Augustine says that the love of God comprises all virtues and perfects all virtuous operations within us. . .[24] Therefore, he who possesses charity, is clothed in a nuptial garment, adorned with every kind of virtue, like Joseph's coat of many colors.[25] Or rather, his perfection is the epitome of all perfections, the perfection of all virtues . . . and without it, it would not only be impossible to possess all virtues in their entirety, but one would not even be able to achieve perfection in any one virtue."[26]

Quite clearly, defects should be avoided and virtues practiced; everything in love and through love. We stand not only with Saint Paul but above all with the Gospel: "Without Me you can do nothing."[27] That also is clear. And so it seems to us that a person acts with greater security if he aims directly at union with Jesus in order to arrive at good works, rather than the opposite, for he can accomplish nothing without Jesus.

That is why Jesus in the Gospel adds: "As the branch cannot bear fruit of itself, unless it abide in the vine, so neither can you, unless you abide in Me. I am the vine; you the branches: He that abideth in Me, and I in him, the

---

23. II, II, 23, 4 ad. 2.
24. *De Moribus Eccl.* ch. 15.
25. Genesis 37:14.
26. *Of the Love of God,* Book II, chapter 8.
27. John 15:5.

same beareth much fruit."[28] And how should we dwell in Jesus so that He can dwell in us? "God is charity: and he that abideth in charity, abideth in God, and God in him."[29] How clear and straightforward everything is in the Gospel! Through love we achieve union with Jesus and through union with Jesus we obtain every fruit of sanctification in abundance, for the virtues flow into the soul just as the sap flows from the vine into the branches.

This truth had its solemn confirmation in the teaching, and even more so in the life of Saint Teresa who, through love, attained every virtue to an heroic degree as the Church has proclaimed. And now it would appear that God desires to confirm that truth anew through the teaching and example of Sister Consolata. For that reason we will append here a few of the instructions which Jesus gave to the humble Capuchin nun in confirmation of this.

Above all, love is the first and most perfect reparation for one's sins. "Repentance which excludes the love of God," teaches Saint Francis de Sales, "is infernal. Repentance which does not reject love but is without it, is imperfect and cannot procure salvation by itself until it has attained to love and has become united with it."[30] After all, we have only to open the Gospel: "Many sins are forgiven her, because she hath loved much." And to remove all doubt in this respect: "To whom less is forgiven, he loveth less."[31] The Gospels are intended for all time and for all souls, just as this teaching of Jesus to Sister Consolata is meant for all souls:

---

28. John 15:4-5.
29. I John 14:16.
30. *Of the Love of God*, Book II, chapter 19.
31. Luke 7:47.

Do you wish to do penance for your sins? Then love Me! Love shall be your penance! (November 22nd, 1935)

The same may be said for those who wish to make reparation for the sins of others. On Palm Sunday 1936, while Sister Consolata was reading the Passion of Our Lord, she paused over the betrayal of Judas:

"Oh, if only I could make reparation for all sacrileges!"

At that she heard: *Yes, with love you can make reparation for the horrible sacrileges; with love you can suffer, you can immolate yourself and can consummate the sacrifice! Everything through love, and only through love!*

Love is not only reparation, but also purification. In fact it is a light which reveals to the soul the slightest defects which lessen its beauty; it is a force which gives the soul the necessary energy to eradicate her defects to the very roots, it is a fire which burns and consumes the noxious weeds which spring up within us. "I know," said Saint Teresa, "that the fire of love is more sanctifying than that of purgatory."

On the evening of November 11th, 1935, Jesus said to Sister Consolata, as she was praying before the tabernacle:

Consolata, offer Me your shortcomings of to-day.

"O Jesus, I cannot recall them!"

I too have forgotten them.

"And so? . . ."

Tell Me that you love Me, and go in peace, for they do not exist any more.

On another day when she humbly confessed herself to be full of deficiencies, Jesus made her understand: *Love Me! Love will make all your deficiencies vanish.* (August 19th, 1935)

As has already been said, Jesus did not wish her to dwell

again on her own infidelities, and so He told her on July 9th, 1934:

Do not always keep looking back at yourself, and on what you have done; but look beyond all those defects, and love always!

After renewing the soul by reparation and purification, love makes her achieve all virtues and become perfect in them. Great was certainly the particular vocation of Sister Consolata, for great were God's designs in her regard. But it was also necessary that she should respond to them. Note how Jesus reassured her on August 30th, 1935:

Do you want to live up to your vocation? Then love Me alone. Love Me always. Then you will be conforming yourself completely to My plans for you!

This naturally requires the exercise of virtue, but it is precisely by means of love that the soul is certain to practice it. Thus, Jesus promised her concerning the love of neighbor which was so dear to her:

You must think only about loving Me, and I will see to it that you become charitable. (July 2nd, 1935)

A similar promise concerned humility, that fundamental virtue of Christian perfection:

The more you will dwell in Me, the more will I let My humility work through you. (August 22nd, 1935)

Love Me alone! I will attend to maintaining you in humility. If you will but dwell in Me, that which is in the vine will also be in the branches. (July 4th, 1935)

It is not therefore as though a soul did not appreciate the value and feel the need of the other virtues when she follows the path of love; she is deeply convinced that the surest means for attaining these virtues is to be closely united to Jesus like the branch to the vine. Hence Jesus' warning to Sister Consolata lest she stray from the right way:

Love is sanctity. The more you love Me, the more you will become holy! (August 20th, 1935)

Remember that love, and only love, will bring you to the highest degree of sanctity! (November 8th, 1935)

At the same time God the Father assured her concerning the summit of sanctity: *Remember, Consolata, that love and only love will bring you victorious to every summit!* (September 19, 1935)

FRUITS OF THE LIFE OF LOVE

We will see later how the soul can put the life of love into actual practice. Here let us briefly mention a few particular fruits which will derive from it besides those already touched upon.

The first is the intimate and profound joy of the soul who knows and feels that she possesses God and is possessed by Him. She knows and feels how she can best utilize the short day of this life for the glory of God, for herself, and for the salvation of souls; she knows and feels that nothing and no one can tear this immense treasure from her, if only she will faithfully persevere on the road she has taken; and so she can make her own the words of the Apostle: "Who then shall separate us from the love of Christ?"[32]

One of the earliest lessons which Jesus taught to Sister Consolata was this:

Love Me, and you will be happy; and the more you

---

32. Romans 8:35.

love Me, the happier you will be! Even when you will find yourself in utter darkness, love will produce light, love will produce strength, and love will produce joy! (March 15th, 1934)

This is true of all souls, but in particular of Religious, the souls chosen and beloved by Christ:

If all My betrothed would love Me, I would pour heaven into their hearts even while they still dwelt upon earth, for heaven is enjoyed by loving Me! (August 20th, 1935)

Oh, that every soul might understand this truth! That this poor world might understand it, which has lost the way to its true and only happiness because it has turned away from Jesus! On October 13th, 1935, Our Lord exclaimed to Sister Consolata:

Oh, if people would only love Me, what felicity would reign in this unhappy world!

And what shall we say about suffering, that heritage of every human creature which is such a mighty means to sanctification? Will the soul who lives for love be spared suffering? On the contrary, love is nourished precisely by sacrifice. Calvary is the very height of sacrifice because it is the ultimate in love. Jesus promised Sister Consolata on May 27th, 1936:

Love will carry you to the height of suffering.

But it is actually not enough to merely suffer; one must suffer well, and this difficult science is learned only in the school of love:

In order to suffer well, you need to love, solely love, always love, and to love intensely! (November 11th, 1935)

Suffering has a supernatural value in proportion to the purity and the depth of the love which gives it life. Hence Jesus told Sister Consolata on December 1st, 1935:

Love is greater than suffering; and suffering will be the more perfect, the more powerful the love which is in you.

It is love, and only love, that can change suffering into joy: "I exceedingly abound with joy in all our tribulation."[33] This Jesus confirmed to Sister Consolata on December 1st, 1935:

When suffering is accepted with love, it is no longer suffering, but is changed into joy.

On October 18th, 1935, God the Father also promised this in exchange for love:

Consolata, I give you the joy of sorrow, and joy in sorrow.

This naturally does not prevent the soul from "feeling" the suffering, nor does it dispense her from making an effort to suffer with perfection. Nevertheless, it is always true that love gives the soul the necessary strength: "Put me as a seal upon thy heart, as a seal upon thine arm, for love is strong as death."[34] And it is even stronger than death, for the soul who loves is invested with divine strength. Sister Consolata was one day bewailing her own infidelity:

"O Jesus, I am so worthless!"

Then unite yourself to strength!

"How can I do that?"

By remaining in love. United to strength, you will be stronger than the strong! (February 26th, 1936)

Another fruit which is equally inseparable from the life of love is a profound and stable peace of soul. Having abandoned herself with complete trust to Love, the soul has by that very fact eliminated the cause of so much unrest which

---

33. II Corinthians 7:4.
34. Canticle of Canticles 8:6.

comes from a multitude of unsatisfied and unattainable desires and from ever searching out new paths, new means, new practices. The soul has simplified her spiritual life to the greatest possible extent. There is now but one desire: to love; but one occupation: to love; she is preoccupied with only one thing: to love. Everything else will come to her through love.

It is not, therefore, a case of quietism or anything of the sort, but the exact opposite; for to live a life of love means to live the supernatural life as intensely as possible and to concentrate upon one point only: love. One of the teachings most often repeated by Jesus to Sister Consolata was this:

You must think only of loving Me! I will think of everything else, even to the smallest details!

In this manner vain thoughts, useless outside interests, oppressing preoccupations, all are eliminated for the soul who lives in love:

Consolata, you know that I am thinking of everything, that I am providing for everything down to the smallest detail. Therefore, do not let one thought enter your mind, not one outside interest. . . Have no fear! I am taking care of you! (July 31, 1936)

Well did she experience this throughout her whole life. When she had been deprived of Our Lord's sensible presence she wrote:

". . . From the day on which Jesus told me: 'I will think of everything, even the smallest details, but you must think only of loving Me,' from that day on He took upon Himself the responsibility for all my duties, my promises, my desires, in short, everything. And even to-day when He is silent, He continues to think of everything, even the minutest details. Jesus acts in me, and Consolata has only to think of loving

Him. Yes, the daily events are matters which must not interest me any more; I must dispose myself to let only things of heaven enter. Heaven consists in loving, and so I must not permit anything but love to enter."

If heaven consists in loving, then the felicity of heaven, as we have already pointed out, is an act of the soul who is living on love. But love on this planet is militant, whereas in heaven it will be jubilant and adoring. Sister Consolata declared herself one day to be unworthy of eternal happiness because it seemed to her that she was doing nothing, but Jesus told her:

You think you do not deserve these joys in eternity because you are doing nothing? Tell Me, what does the catechism say? That you have been created to love Me, to serve Me, and to be happy with Me in all eternity. And you, do you not love Me? Do you not serve Me? Well, then you are entitled to the glory and joy of heaven! I give you heaven not only out of love, but out of justice. (November 15th, 1935)

And what heaven? For an answer we cite another quotation from Sister Consolata's diary (May 1935):

". . . This evening I remained for a few minutes in the laundry to do an act of charity. While I was at work grace whispered into my heart, all filled with kindly thoughts: 'You will see, you will see, what I will be able to do with Consolata! You love Me, and I will give you all the glory!' 'Jesus, you will also give me all the suffering, will you not?' 'Yes, all the suffering, all the love, and all the glory, because you love Me! . . .'"

If we understand the doctrine rightly which Jesus here showed to Sister Consolata, then love does not take our faculties and operations and apply to them an external label, but love vivifies everything from within by providing a new form of life and a new perfection. This has its roots in grace, which is the seed of glory. When we conclude, therefore, that this gift invests the totality of the present and the future life (suffering, love, glory), we are merely translating this perfect work of charity into the subject which we love.

How can one still doubt that love is everything, that it gives all to Jesus and receives all from Him? In concluding, therefore, this chapter on the life of love, we will have this chosen creature who believed in Love, who hoped and confided in Love, who loved Love, give expression to the seraphic ardor of her heart:

"O Jesus, I too will sing, always sing; in the hour of battle as well as in the hour of love; in the hour of joy, as in the hour of sorrow. Thus, precisely thus, be my life consumed: in loving Thee, and in sacrificing myself. And my canticle of love, my weak sacrifices, will acquire infinite merit through Thy Heart. Oh yes, I feel that Consolata will be an apostle of Thy Heart, of Thy mercy, always, even to the end of time! Thou hast told me so Thyself, O Jesus! . . . Jesus, I do believe; I believe, and I confide in Thee! . . . Jesus, I love Thee!"

- IV -

LIVING AN ACT OF PERFECT LOVE

TO live a life of love means to see to it that love truly becomes the very life of the soul, that the heart, the mind, one's strength, everything, is always employed in loving the good God. "Thou shalt love the Lord thy God with thy whole heart, and with thy whole soul, and with thy whole mind, and with thy whole strength."[1] In other words, it means carrying into perfect execution that other precept of the divine Master: "As the Father hath loved Me, I also have loved you. Abide in My love!"[2] To *abide* signifies a continuous action; *in love*, not in the simple state of grace, but in affective and effective love; *in My love*, in the love of Jesus as an expression also of our love for His and our Father.

In practice, in the divine instructions given to Sister Consolata, this all amounts to an effort of the soul to transform her own life into an act of perfect love; not only to perform all actions with love, not only to gather and offer up with

---

1. Mark 12:30.
2. John 15:9.

love the flowers of small sacrifices and small acts of virtue, but to make an effort to enliven every instant of this short earthly journey with love.

What is perfect love? It is above all a pure love with which one loves God for His own sake. It is also *actual* love which is undoubtedly more perfect than habitual love. It is a love, therefore, which embraces God and souls in the same heartbeat, for it is impossible to love God without loving one's neighbor. We should also add that our love for Jesus cannot and must not ever be separated from our love for the Blessed Virgin, for we cannot please Jesus if we do not also love His and our Mother. Nor will our love reach God in true perfection unless it is made to pass through the love of Mary, the one and only creature who has ever loved God here below in the way He wishes to be loved and ought to be loved.

If a formula for perfect love is desired, it must therefore comprise, together with the love of Jesus, also the love of Our Lady and of all souls. Such is precisely the formula for the act of love which Jesus communicated to Sister Consolata, for transmittal to all souls.

THE CONVENIENCE OF A FORMULA

It is understandable that the majority of souls will require the aid of some practical, short, and easy formula to serve as an expression of their own love and so facilitate an intimacy of love with Jesus.

Just as a mother will bend over her little child in an act of love and tell him over and over again that word, that phrase, which he should repeat in returning her affection, so did Jesus deign to bend down over a very tiny soul, Sister Consolata, in order to dictate to her and then require from her that unceasing act of love which from then on was to constitute the very essence of her spiritual life and the principal means for realizing her vocation to love, her very life of love.

THE FORMULA FOR THE UNCEASING ACT OF LOVE

The act of love which Jesus dictated to Sister Consolata is worded as follows:

Jesus, Mary, I love You! Save souls!

It will be of benefit to souls to examine the intrinsic value of this act of love, at least briefly:

1. It would be impossible to formulate a more *perfect* act of love in fewer words, for it contains everything: love of Jesus, love of Mary, and love of souls.

2. This is an act of *pure* love, for by it one gives to God the most excellent gift of all: love and souls.

3. At the same time it is an act of *perfect charity* for in it the love of one's neighbor finds its highest expression in an unceasing prayer for the benefit of souls; and it comprises all souls, including those in purgatory, and all their needs, as explained by Jesus Himself.

4. This act of love is, therefore, a synthesis of the two great commandments which are in turn the very essence of the Law.

5. Because this act is unceasing in the sense which we

will now explain, it brings the soul to a literal and perfect fulfillment of the first commandment which is, to love God *with all one's heart;* the act of love must spring from the heart, for it is the heart that loves with the greatest possible continuity and intensity: *with the whole mind;* the continuity of the act of love precludes of itself every useless voluntary thought: *with the whole soul,* that is, as Saint Thomas explains, with all one's will; the unceasing act of love is sustained by the fervor of the will, not by sentiment: *with one's whole strength;* in order to attain the greatest possible continuity and intensity of love, it is necessary to concentrate all the soul's energies upon it.

Saint Francis de Sales writes: "Man is the perfection of the universe, the soul is the perfection of man, and love is the perfection of the soul... Hence the love of God is the end, the perfection, and the ultimate beauty of the universe. This is what gives greatness and supremacy to the divine commandment which the Saviour calls the first and great commandment. That commandment is like a sun which illumines and gives dignity to all the holy laws, the divine precepts, and all the sacred Scriptures. Everything was created for that heavenly love, and everything is related to it. From the sacred trunk of this commandment have sprung all the counsels, the exhortations, the inspirations, and the other commandments, like blossoms from the same tree, and its fruit is life eternal. It is a great commandment, and its perfect execution carries over into life eternal—in fact it is life eternal itself."[3]

6. The act of love is in itself and in the above formula also a *prayer,* in fact it is the most perfect of prayers, for it

---

3. *Of the Love of God,* Book 10, chapter 1.

brings the soul to a literal and perfect execution of that other evangelical precept: "We ought always to pray, and not to faint."[4]

7. Through this act of love the soul lives a *supernatural life* as intensely as possible for the glory of God, for her own sanctification, and for the salvation of souls.

8. Through it the soul lives an *essentially mortified life*, by excluding everything else in silent self-dedication. Thus she comes to join the ranks of the *little victims of love*.

In the following we will see in what the divine favors and promises consist which accompany the unceasing act of love.

HOW THE UNCEASING ACT OF LOVE IS TO BE UNDERSTOOD

The instructions which Jesus gave to Sister Consolata concerning the unceasing act of love establish its far-reaching importance and prevent one from falling into simple errors.

It would be wrong, for instance, to mistake the act of love for a mere ejaculation, to be recited more or less frequently in preference to others. That would not be a bad thing, and for the majority of souls it may even be sufficient, but this would not correspond to the divine intention. Our Lord did not intend to suggest a new ejaculation, but to point out to souls a spiritual way which would make the life of love easy for them. If then the act of love is to be a way of life for the soul, then it follows that the act ought

---

4. Luke 18:1.

to be unceasing, at least by an effort of the will, in order to become like the breathing of the soul.

Another point which needs to be made clear is how the continuity of the act of love is to be understood as regards one's daily occupations and diverse duties. Jesus Himself explained this. On Holy Saturday 1934 He promised Sister Consolata His divine assistance and encouraged her to be faithful to the act of love; to that end He suggested to her the following practical form which is applicable to all souls:

Consolata, just as I have taken on the responsibility for your thoughts and words, so also for your continuous act of love. But you must remember once and for all that when you are conversing with Me or when you are writing or meditating, the act of love continues. I credit you with it just the same even though the heart is obliged to keep silent at those times!

It is clear, therefore, that the unceasing act of love does not interfere with the community life and the regular life of the one who practices it. It is not detrimental to other acts of piety, whether of obligation or free will. It does not hinder one's daily occupations, nor can it in turn be hindered by them. Only the soul must be intent upon continuing her song of love in the measure allowed by the nature of her occupation.

A third observation is equally important: the unceasing act of love must not be a superficial thing, a mechanical repetition of a formula, but rather a true canticle of love. In fact—and this must be stressed—it is not even necessary that the act be pronounced with the lips. An act of love is not a simple spoken phrase but an interior act of the mind which thinks of loving, and of the will which desires to love, and so loves. Thus the unceasing act of love is a continuous, silent effusion of love. The formula, one must remember, is no more than an aid which enables the soul to concentrate more easily upon love, upon perfect love.

In the life of the servant of God, Father Adolph Petit, S.J., we read: "When someone inquired of him about some means for nourishing this love, he would reply: 'I know of but one, to love. Just as one learns to read by reading, and to write by writing, so does one learn to love Our Lord by multiplying one's acts of love for Him. Each one of these acts is as it were an armful of kindling, to be thrown on the fire; it renders the flame of love more ardent.'"

This is also what Jesus told Sister Consolata on November 16th, 1935, and His words may well serve as an introduction to the doctrine of the unceasing act of love:

If a creature of good will desires to love Me and to make of her life one single act of love from the moment of her rising until she falls asleep at night—from the heart, be it well understood—then I will perform incredible things for that soul. Write that down!

It is with the heart, therefore, that one must be unceasingly loving. And that, we repeat, does not mean that the soul must *feel* delight or sweetness in doing so, nor must she feel herself to be loving. It suffices to desire to love. Saint Francis de Sales writes that the desire to love is love, both being dependent on the same will.[5] Not only that, but "one always loves perfectly when one eliminates whatever might be a hindrance to giving oneself entirely to God."[6]

---

5. *Of the Love of God,* I, 1-5, II, 16.
6. Saint Thomas, II, II, 184, 2.

THE DIVINE REQUESTS FOR THE UNCEASING ACT OF LOVE

"From the time of my very first spiritual exercises among the Capuchin nuns," writes Sister Consolata, "Jesus asked from my soul that which He later continued to demand from me: the unceasing act of love. He fixed the goal I was to attain, and He assured me that in the light of that love all obstacles, every passion, and every defect would be eradicated. *Nothing must detach you from the continuous act of love,* He told me during meditation on the day of my clothing. And later, during Holy Communion: *I ask only this of you: a continuous act of love!* At the beginning it was: *Jesus, I love Thee!* Later He desired me to add: *Jesus, Mary, I love You!* And finally He wanted it completed thus: *Jesus, Mary, I love You! Save souls!*"

From that moment on there were countless divine requests for the act of love. We hope we will be pardoned for giving numerous quotations even at the risk of repetition. It is a matter of the greatest importance and constitutes as it were the very justification for this new divine message. Everything we have said so far about the life of love, though most useful and in a certain measure necessary, would only have a relative value because already found in substance in the lives and writings of other privileged souls, were it not integrated with the revelation and doctrine of the act of love. For the sake of brevity we will print here the various divine requests, or at least those which we have at hand, for Sister Consolata's diary is not yet available in its entirety.

The first request is of March 15th, 1934:
Love Me, Consolata; your act of love delights Me!
Jesus did not only recommend it, He required it (October 15th, 1934):
Consolata, I have certain rights over you; therefore, I desire from you an unceasing 'Jesus, Mary, I love You! Save souls!' from the time you awaken in the morning to when you go to sleep in the evening! I require it!

And as though in answer to a spontaneous difficulty of the poor creature, He added:
If you believe Me to be omnipotent, then you must also believe Me to be capable of granting you this continual act of love. I will it!

The act of love was, therefore, to become the vital nourishment for the soul:
As a little fish will die outside of water, so also will you, outside the act of love! (June 23rd, 1935)

On the other hand, just as the fish keeps alive in water and develops, so also was the life of grace to develop and become perfect through the unceasing act of love and the perfecting of charity in her, until it achieved that complete divesting and annihilating of herself which is a mystical death:
You must live in self-effacement and enveloped in one single and continual 'Jesus, Mary, I love you! Save souls!' Nothing else! No one and nothing else must exist for you, only the act of love! (October 25th, 1935)

This mystical death is not quietism, but a transition to the heroic life, for now He no longer finds any obstacles to His divine workings and so can act in the soul as her uncontested sovereign:
Upon your self-denial I will build up My marvelous

work.⁷ *And do you know what can procure your self-effacement? The unceasing act of love! Nothing remains of yourself or for yourself, but through the unceasing act of love all is for Me!* (September 7th, 1935)

Jesus desired her soul to become so absorbed in this continual act of love as to become identified with it and transformed into it:

Saint John the Baptist called himself 'a voice crying in the wilderness.' You are to be "an unceasing act of love!' (April 3rd, 1936)

No creature was to distract her, therefore, from her one duty:

Duc in altum! Launch out into the deep!⁸ Bid farewell forever to all that is earth and creature, and head for the open sea with the unceasing act of love! Forward! Toward the eternal shores! (June 28th, 1936)

She was to devote all her spiritual energies to this single purpose:

Consolata, in order not to lose time, you should renew all your promises every time you pronounce an act of love. If you have fallen, raise yourself up again; if you have forgotten, then start anew; an act of love is useful for everything, at any time, and under every condition! (December 3rd, 1935)

And because Sister Consolata was accustomed to renew her particular vows daily during Holy Communion, Jesus suggested to her on May 30th, 1936:

Be extremely vigilant not to permit one thought to enter, not to utter a single sentence except in reply; but do not lose

---

7. In what this work consists, will be explained further on.
8. Luke 5:4.

yourself in this effort. No! Lose yourself rather in the unceasing act of love!

This divine requirement of observing a rigorous silence aimed precisely at maintaining Sister Consolata in this continuity of love:

It does not suffice for you to avoid talking during recreation. What I desire is the continual act of love! That is why I require silence from you! (September 8th, 1936)

Naturally, the enemy raged against this unceasing act of love and tried by every means to raise doubts in Sister Consolata's soul regarding the path she was following; but Jesus reassured her with these words:

Whatever disturbs you in your act of love, does not come from Me! (April 5th, 1936)

In short, Jesus desired her to be heroic in the continuity of her love so as to attain to the greatest possible perfection:

It is My desire that, throughout your day, you should not deny Me one single act of love, not even one! Do you understand? (July 31st, 1936)

By means of the unceasing act of love Sister Consolata was to realize her particular vocation, her mission on behalf of her Brothers and her own sanctification, everything! On the First Friday of February 1935 Jesus told her:

Forget everything else! Love Me continuously, even though your heart be of ice or stone. That does not matter. But everything depends upon an unceasing act of love, and upon nothing else!

And clearer still, on December 16th, 1935:

You must give to Jesus the one thing He wishes to draw from your vocation, and that is the unceasing act of love, no matter in what state your soul may happen to be!

Jesus was eager and insistent to keep Sister Consolata steadfast in the continuity of her love under all spiritual conditions. To love without "feeling" is an interior martyrdom, and many a soul abstains from making acts of love when in that spiritual state for fear that they would not be truthful. That is the enemy's crafty trick to hinder the soul from loving. Saint Francis de Sales writes: "To say to God 'I love Thee' is something we ought never to leave undone, even though we may have no lively feeling of love, for we do have the will and the great desire to love Him!" Naturally, in that case, the continuity of love means an effort against nature, and so it was also in the case of Sister Consolata against whom the enemy unleashed all manner of attacks. To put her on her guard, Jesus told her on October 10th, 1935:

Consolata, it matters little that the devil and your passions unleash in your soul every possible attack; do not mind thunder, storm, and lightning. Say to yourself: 'I want to continue undismayed my act of love from one Communion to the next; that is my duty, my sole duty!' And so, forward! Nothing else!

Enlisted under the banner of unceasing love, Sister Consolata had, in her struggle for sanctity, to defend it with the same valor as the good soldier defends the flag of his country:

The unceasing act of love is your flag. Defend it against the enemy at the cost of your life! (September 6th, 1936)

One must love one's flag; one must defend it at all costs, live under it, and die clutching it to one's heart, so that it may never fall into enemy hands. Do the same with your act of love! Even if it costs you an effort, give it to Me without ceasing! (September 7th, 1936)

If she happened to interrupt the act out of human weakness, she was not to become discouraged on account of that, much less to abandon the struggle:

Raise your effort to the highest pitch and, firmly determined not to lose one single act of love, take up the struggle again without wasting a backward glance at the interruption!

The continuity of love was not, therefore, an infused gift for Sister Consolata. True, she had special graces inherent in her mission, but she had to correspond to them always with an heroic effort of the will, without stopping when the conflict became more bitter, and without losing courage over her more or less voluntary infidelities. To this Jesus spurred her on by saying:

Love Me, Consolata, without regard to the struggle and your inevitable falls. Try not to be impressed by a fall, but continue unperturbed in your act of love! (September 7th, 1936)

Make every effort, Consolata; it is for your own good! It is upon the effort that I now insist, that you offer Me unceasingly an act of love! (September 8th, 1936)

Certainly, Jesus might have brought her in one stride to the desired peak, but He did not wish to do so. He told her quite clearly on September 16th, 1936—and this should be a lesson and encouragement to all souls:

Do you think I could not grant you this continuity of love? It pleases Me to see you struggle, fall, and rise again, in short, making an effort. I like to see what you can do. And do you know what delights Me most? It is when you rise above everything unperturbed and continue your act of love!

Jesus never concealed from her (as we will see later), that the continual act of love would come to be a cross for her soul because it employed all the faculties of the soul in one continuous effort and destroyed everything in the creature, even a useless thought. To encourage her on that difficult path, He suggested that she give no thought to the future but live and sanctify the present moment with love:

Live by loving, one minute at a time! An entire day is too long for you!

In addition Jesus promised His constant support and that of her spiritual director:

Have no fear, Consolata, when your act of love is impeded by your insistent struggle, I will send you your spiritual director, so that you will not have to stop or delay your ascent; but you must do nothing but love continuously, even if it costs an effort, for only the continual act of love will give you the strength you need for everything! (October 14th, 1935)

One day Jesus taught Sister Consolata how she could render valuable, through an act of love, even the brief intervals between versicles and antiphones, etc., while in choir, but she doubted whether her heart would be able to sustain so intense an activity. Jesus replied:

I will strengthen it with Mine!

Above all, Jesus promised her that He would make good all deficiencies of her weak nature:

You must do your utmost to offer Me the unceasing act of love; but when you fail, I will make it good. No, have no fear, I am always kind!

Therefore, Our Lord's entire workings in Sister Consolata's soul aimed at bringing her to a continuity of love and maintaining her in it. When she wondered one day whether Jesus had not exhausted His vocabulary for His customary demand, she was answered:

Have no fear that I have exhausted the phrases with

which to ask of you the same thing: love! I am omnipotent, and am able to repeat the same demand unto infinity in ever changing phraseology!

Another time, when she was astonished that Jesus had not yet tired of the same demand, she heard this reply:

No, I am not tired of it, nor will I ever tire of it, for I desire only this one thing: that you should love Me! Nothing else!

THE SPIRITUAL FRUITFULNESS
OF THE UNCEASING ACT OF LOVE

Who brings souls to salvation? Not we, certainly! It is Jesus Crucified who has been saving souls and continues to save them by applying the infinite merits of His bloody expiation. At the most, and due to His condescension, we can become co-operators in the salvation of souls in proportion to our union with Him, that is, our love for Him.

Everything that Saint Paul says about love as related to the supernatural value of our actions, may be applied to our apostolate for the benefit of other souls. Without love, all our words, whether spoken or written, would be but sounding brass and tinkling cymbals; all our knowledge would profit us nothing, nor would our endeavors to find new ways of impressing souls. We may be preachers, public speakers, journalists, organizers, but if the charity of Our Lord does not burn within us, we will never be apostles. An apostle is one who speaks and acts in the Name of Jesus, is in intimate union with Him, is inflamed by the same love for God the Father and the same passionate zeal for saving souls.

Little Saint Teresa loved Jesus like a seraph and had the soul of an apostle. Not only that, but through love she exercised so real, so great, and so universal an apostolate as to be proclaimed Patroness of the Missions, though she never saw a mission country and never preached a sermon. The one who proclaimed her was the Church, which is guided by the Holy Spirit, who is God. This solemn lesson which God gave the world was not understood by all; but it is finding its confirmation to-day in the life of Sister Consolata. She too was burning with zeal because inflamed with love; she too has been given a copious harvest of souls in reward for her love. Here is what Jesus told her concerning the apostolic fruitfulness of the act of love:

Remember that one act of love may decide the eternal salvation of a soul! You ought to feel remorse, therefore, over the omission of a single 'Jesus, Mary, I love You! Save souls!' (October 8th, 1935)

The same consoling promise was given her at other times:

Do not lose time! Every act of love means a soul!

The Blessed Virgin also exhorted her in the same sense concerning the unceasing act of love:

"Only in heaven will you come to know its value and its fruitfulness in saving souls!"

For a number of years Sister Consolata had been praying for the conversion of her brother Nicholas and for that of her uncle Felix Viano. The former surrendered to grace at Easter 1936, and in the month of July following Jesus told her:

Remember, Consolata, that I have not given you Nicholas, nor will I give you your uncle Felix, in reward for your penances and sacrifices, but solely because of your unceasing act of love. Remember that, for it is love that I desire from My creatures!

Nicholas died a holy death in December 1947.

The act of love is also most fruitful as a prayer of reparation:

Why is it, Consolata, that I do not permit you so many vocal prayers? It is because the act of love is more fruitful. One 'Jesus, Mary, I love You! Save souls!' repairs a thousand blasphemies! (October 8th, 1935)

The unceasing act of love also has greater value for the soul who is practicing it and is, therefore, more fruitful of merit than any other work:

Consolata, place at one side all the acts of virtue which you could perform to-day, and on the other side a single day passed in a continuous act of love—I will prefer the day passed in continual love to anything else you might do or offer Me!

Hence, every time Sister Consolata resolved to offer to Jesus or Our Lady some particular homage, grace intervened and solicited an act of love from her instead. In preparation for the feast of the Immaculate Conception, 1935, Jesus suggested:

What would you like to give your heavenly Mother during her Novena? Offer her a continual 'Jesus, Mary, I love You! Save souls!' With that you will be giving her everything!

Lastly, the act of love is most fruitful in the matter of sanctifying the soul precisely because through it we not only give everything to Jesus, but we also receive everything from Him. In commenting on the words of the Gospel "without Me you can do nothing," Jesus told her on October 26th, 1935:

This is for you the most comforting saying in the Gospel, because it excuses all your weaknesses and throws you in complete abandonment upon the Heart of God. There, dissolved in a single act of love, you may ask what you will, and it will be granted you!

For Jesus will not permit Himself to be outdone in generosity by His poor creature who is intent on loving Him continually:

Oh, remain fixed in this one resolve, not to interrupt the act of love! That suffices for Me. Remain faithful to it, renew it hour by hour, and I will grant you everything, Consolata, truly everything! (September 13th, 1936)

The soul who is faithful to the unceasing act of love will in truth be most faithful in everything else, as God the Father promised Sister Consolata on September 23rd, 1935:

Look, Consolata, concentrate on your resolve to love continuously! This includes all other resolutions. If you observe this one, you will be observing all the others!

Jesus gave her the reason for this:

Each of your acts of love draws faithfulness into your being, for it draws Me, Who am Faithfulness itself! (July 14th, 1936)

Thus established in fidelity to all her duties and resolutions, the soul will be victorious over her passions and her enemies:

In order to always gain the victory, only one thing is necessary: never to omit one act of love! (May 30th, 1936)

Abundant will also be the fruit for sanctification:

You have effaced yourself as regards your spiritual director and have shut yourself up in the one word 'obey!' Now obliterate yourself in Me and shut yourself up in the one phrase: 'Jesus, Mary, I love You! Save souls!' You will gather much fruit! (October 26th, 1935)

Above all, the unceasing act of love will render the soul ready for every sacrifice asked of her:

Look, Consolata, concentrate upon one continual 'Jesus Mary, I love You! Save souls!' It is the one and only resolution which will give you the strength to reply with a 'yes' to My every request for sacrifice! (September 24th, 1935)

And again, on December 1st, 1935:

Do you know why I tell you to continue solely in this way? It is because by keeping you always united to Me, this continuity of love makes you ready for everything at any moment.

In order to suffer well, it is necessary to love deeply, as has already been said. It is an illusion to believe otherwise. A little experience with other souls and with one's own is sufficient to prove that it is not sacrifice which brings one to love (oh, how many souls do not suffer well!), but it is love which brings one to sacrifice, that is, to a sacrifice which is accepted, carried out, and offered up with joy and thanksgiving. Such a sacrifice then becomes food for love. That is why Jesus told Sister Consolata on October 19th, 1935:

Consolata, prepare yourself for suffering through love. Love continuously! Alas, if you were ever to cease loving!

Jesus reminded her frequently of her status of victim-soul in order to induce her to persevere in the continuity of her love. Thus on November 24th, 1935:

I know that the continual act of love costs you something, particularly at certain times. But it is more meritorious so, Consolata! And then you must never forget that I have chosen you to be a victim of love!

We will see in the following chapter how this victim state was realized in Sister Consolata through the unceasing act of love, and how it made the solemn promise come true which Jesus made her one day:

Consolata, I swear that I will lead you to every height of love and of sorrow; but as for you: 'Jesus, Mary, I love You! Save souls!' Nothing else!

- V -

PERFECTING THE LIFE OF LOVE THROUGH PERFECTING THE UNCEASING ACT OF LOVE

PREMISE

A few words are necessary here in order that souls who wish to follow Sister Consolata and strive for that highest perfection in the way of love to which God called her, do not become frightened and conclude that it is something impossible and not meant for them.

Let us note, therefore, in the first place: we ought not to be astonished that Jesus should have called a soul to the highest perfection; for He has let us know through the Gospel: "Be you therefore perfect, as also your heavenly Father is perfect."[1] An impossible goal? And yet it was proposed to us by Jesus Himself, and it teaches us that on the path to sanctification the soul never reaches a point where she may slacken her efforts. We are not dispensed from striving toward the peak with all our strength, even though it be impossible to attain it.

---

1. Matthew 5:48.

In the second place it must be observed that, just because Jesus proposed such a sublime height to Sister Consolata, this does not imply that she attained it absolutely and definitely so that there remained nothing more for her to do. We have pointed out again and again that throughout her entire life she never laid down her weapons in the good fight, and this stands to prove that she never felt herself to have reached the loftiest peak, though the one she did attain was certainly very high.

From this it follows—and this is the third observation—that with God it is not so much the success which counts, for that depends solely upon Him, but rather the earnest and determined effort made by the creature in the relentless struggle, always sustained by grace, for that must not be lacking. This grace, however, is not granted to all in equal measure, but in accordance with God's merciful designs. Now, since Sister Consolata was chosen by God to show the world the road to the unceasing act of love, it is easy to understand why God should have favored her with extraordinary graces in proportion to her vocation and mission, so as to present her as a model to all souls who would be called to follow her.

It is clear, therefore, that the divine demands, as contained in the present chapter, must not be thought to apply in the same measure to all souls, even among those who are called to follow the same path. It suffices for them to keep their eyes fixed upon the model supplied them by God in Sister Consolata, to respond generously to grace, to try to imitate her to the best of their ability, and to keep always in mind that God does not reward the result but the effort.

CONTINUITY OF LOVE IN THE UNCEASING ACT OF LOVE

Besides the purity with which one loves God for His own sake, the perfection of love consists above all in its effective continuity, in actual love, not merely habitual love. That must, therefore, be the goal toward which the soul should strive if she wishes to perfect herself more and more in the life of love. And how can such a continuity be achieved? Jesus uses Sister Consolata to point out to us the practical means, one which is accessible to all souls of good will: the unceasing act of love.

On August 22nd, 1935, He told her quite clearly:

Through your contact with Me, which results from the act of love, you will discern the little defects which might tend to detach you from this divine union, and you will drive them away. In this manner your entire day will become one continual throb of love from the moment you arise until you fall asleep, and it will even continue into eternity.

At another time Our Lord referred to the fact that she was enjoying His sensible presence in her heart (she beheld Him intellectually under the form of the Sacred Heart or as the Crucified Christ):

Not only is your cell for you a sanctuary where you can always find Jesus, the Sacred Heart or the Crucified, but you yourself should be a tabernacle wherever you may be. And just as you do not wish anything but the continual act of love to enter into your cell, so too you must not permit anything but the continual act of love to occupy you, no matter where you may be or in what work you may be engaged. (October 29th, 1935)

The norm of silence which Jesus had suggested to her had no other purpose, as we have already pointed out, than to insure the continuity of the act of love. In speaking of recreation, He said:

You see, Consolata, as long as you dwell in Me by the continual act of love, you are living a marvelous, divine life. Then you believe in all the future which has been revealed to you, and no doubt can then disturb your soul. But if you leave Me during recreation and become involved in conversation with creatures, then you too will feel yourself to be merely a poor creature; and after recreation a doubt will enter your soul whether all these great things which you are experiencing in yourself, might not be an illusion. Therefore, you must never again leave Me for a creature, not even for twenty minutes! Love Me in your heart even while you are giving a needed reply. (November 12th, 1935)

Here one might well ask to what point Sister Consolata carried the continuity of her love. For a human being, an effective and absolute continuity is not possible without being especially privileged by God, as was the case with the Blessed Virgin Mary: "The most glorious Virgin," writes Saint Bernardine de Bustis, "actually loved God continuously and always through a singular privilege." Saint Joseph may also have been blessed in this way, but in a different degree of intensity. As for Sister Consolata, we would say that, just as Jesus never tired of asking from her the unceasing act of love, so she never omitted an effort to respond as perfectly as possible to the divine request.

Speaking of the continuity of the act of love in her diary under the date of September 16th, 1935, she records the following words of Jesus:

You see, since the day of your clothing you have not yet succeeded in giving Me always that which I have requested. On some days, yes, but only on a few.

From this we can see that, five years after her clothing, Sister Consolata had succeeded in actually offering Jesus the act of love on certain days without ceasing. If there were still some gaps on the greater number of days, they were of very short duration and hardly ever voluntary. Nevertheless, even these had to disappear, for Jesus added:

Now, what do you need in order to give Me this continual act of love? You need the twofold silence of thought and word toward everyone, and to see and treat Me in everyone. I will think through you, I will speak through you, I will write through you, but you must be intent solely on loving Me, and loving Me always! That should be your one and only thought from the time of your rising in the morning until you fall asleep at night.

Jesus insisted particularly on purity of mind as being necessary for practicing the unceasing act of love, and explained:

The act of love is like a train traveling along on its track; but if the track is cluttered up with useless thoughts, then the train cannot go on but must come to a stop. You see then how necessary the immaculate purity of mind is for you! So, not another thought, not even one! But what peace results from this, Consolata, is it not true? I alone must be in your mind! (November 25th, 1935)

The soul who has consecrated herself to Love through the unceasing act of love must, therefore, put this external and internal silence into practice without scruples but with generosity and firmness. She must keep ever present the thought of how precious a thing an act of love is, and how the words which Jesus addressed to Sister Consolata on September 13th, 1935, apply also to her:

Consolata, I have consecrated all the time which remains to you in this life into one single act of love. Now, if you were to stop loving in order to follow some other thought or utter some sentence which is not strictly necessary, you would be committing a theft of love!

Such a perfect continuity of love gradually establishes in the soul a state of immolation. Jesus did not conceal this from Sister Consolata:

Consolata, Jesus took the Cross upon His shoulders and proceeded to Calvary. Do you know in what your cross consists? In not losing one act of love! From now on this shall be your one and only program! The act of love itself is not a cross, but never to omit one under any circumstances, that is a cross. However, it will aid you in carrying all other crosses.

I give you as your cross never to lose one single 'Jesus, Mary, I love You! Save souls!' But I also give you the grace to carry this cross faithfully until your dying day. I love you, Consolata. This cross which I lay upon your shoulders, destroys everything in you and brings you at the same time to a scrupulous observance of every little point in your rule, the constitution, and the directives. (November 15th, 1935)

Jesus returned to the same thought on the next day and added:

Do you like the cross which I have bestowed on you? Are you content? . . . You must know that it is a very fruitful one! The cross of love is more fruitful than any other cross for Me and for souls.

It is precisely by means of this silent but ceaseless immolation of love that Sister Consolata achieved her status of a victim of love. She offered herself as a victim in response to a divine request on the day of her solemn profession, April 8th, 1934, but Jesus did not officially consecrate her as a victim until the First Friday in December, 1935. How did this come about, and what were her obligations? Simply this: Jesus confirmed her solemnly in the continuity of love, and she gave her consent.

On the eve of the First Friday, during the Holy Hour, Jesus told her, in preparation for the new act of consecration:

Consolata, does not My thirst for love and My request for reparation for your Brothers and Sisters tell you everything? Yes, I have given you everything; now you must give Me everything: all your love, your every heartbeat, in one unceasing act of love. I desire nothing else, for only by that unceasing act of love do you give Me everything, everything, for yourself and for your Brothers. Here is where I wish you to show Me your fidelity and generosity by completely renouncing every thought, every word, so as never to interrupt your act of love. You must love Me always and accept all consequences, but never interrupt the act of love! I know that this will gradually consume and immolate My Consolata... That is what it means to be a victim of love!

Then, as reply to the natural perplexity of the victim who was pained by her little involuntary infidelities to love and feared she would not fully correspond to the divine plan, Jesus added with divine tenderness:

No, Consolata, no! My omnipotence is great, and grace will enable you to give Me what I ask of you! Do you wish My blessing in order to free your will and render you tenacious in persevering to the end without ever again interrupting this act of love with a thought or a word? So be it! I give you My blessing! You will never again interrupt it! That is My gift to you on this First Friday in December.

On the following morning Jesus carried out the consecration He had announced. But everything took place within the very depth of her soul, and nothing extraordinary showed itself externally. Jesus told her:

This day do I consecrate you as a victim of love. I do not wound you with a dart, but I inflame you in silence. Now you can no longer interrupt your act of love even if you wished to! What time is left you to live from to-day to your last hour, is united with this unceasing act of love. Believe Me, with that you give Me everything! Yes, Consolata, we will despise and trample under foot every obstacle, and we will love always and unceasingly until your last breath. . . Yes, for that I will be responsible!

The responsibilty which Jesus assumed for the continuity of her love did not mean that her soul was in peaceful possession of that continuity. That could never be. Nevertheless, enveloped by the consecrating flame of love, she henceforth felt herself stronger in the holocaust of love. In fact, she thought herself ready to vow the unceasing act of love on the feast of the Sacred Heart, 1936. Jesus had desired it, and she prepared herself with a fervent Novena and meditated each day on one of Father Mateo Crawley's discourses for Religious. A vow of this kind was certainly not to be taken lightly, that she knew well. For she daily experienced what it cost nature not to lose one act of love throughout one whole day. At the beginning of her Novena she wrote (June 10th, 1936):

"This morning I was alone in the workroom, but I felt myself united with the Heart of Jesus. Though longing to bind myself to Him officially by a vow, never to lose an act of love (after receiving permission from my spiritual director), my nature tried to resist this vow which would crucify it completely. I began to understand that the unceasing act of love gives everything to God because it immolates all thoughts, words, imaginings, etc. . . It is death to nature."

Here was not a case of passing enthusiasm, but the consciousness of a tormenting vow, of which she received confirmation from Jesus Himself. One June 13th, during one of the above mentioned discourses, her spirit was struck by this passage: "Be valiant like Mary Most Holy; learn to sing, especially when you are crucified with Jesus." At the same time she heard Jesus whispering in her heart:

That is the way I desire you to be, and for that reason you will bind yourself to Me with a vow, never to lose one act of love, on Friday, when Love will immolate you completely. That is the way I wish you to be, always to be!

On the evening of June 18th, the vigil of the feast, she offered the momentous vow:

". . . This evening, while in choir, the Blessed Sacrament was exposed. The thought occurred to me that one offers gifts on the eve of a feast. Tomorrow is His feast, that of the Sacred Heart. . . The meditation spoke of a Heart which had loved me so much, and from whom It received nothing but ingratitude. My soul, I confess, was not ready to offer the vow which had been asked of me. . . I implored the aid of my holy patrons and then, through the intercession of my Immaculate Mother and Saint Joseph, and with complete trust in the Heart of Jesus, I vowed the unceasing act of love which was to continue without relaxation, even at table, at work, or at recreation. . . Then an innermost and tranquil joy flooded my soul, and a confidence that it would be given me to persevere, and many other blessings. Jesus, I trust in Thee!"

Note the extent which Sister Consolata gave to her vow, that the act of love should be so continuous as never to be relaxed at any time of the day. That certainly requires a particular call from God, which is just what the vocation to love is, and a very special grace! He could not deny it to this soul whom He had chosen for the purpose of showing the world the doctrine and practice of the unceasing act of love.

This does not detract from the fact that her vow was something more than simply bearing the cross: it meant remaining on the cross so as to complete the holocaust of love there. On May 23rd, 1936, Sister Consolata writes:

"To-day I felt a continual thirst for suffering, and this evening, on going to rest, I heard these words: *Oh, if you could know the great value of one act of love!* . . . I came to understand that I will be consumed by the unceasing act of love, and so everything will be accomplished."

That was indeed the case, and after her vow Jesus told her so:

Now it is no more a case of carrying the cross, but of living upon the cross and of persevering on the cross with the unceasing act of love. Courage, Consolata! (July 8th, 1936)

All this required heroism, but Sister Consolata was not one to dread the summit.

"Is my faithfulness to the unceasing act of love heroic? No. Then what ought I to do to make it so?" The divine reply was: *You must will, strongly will, always will it to be so!* (September 16th, 1936)

This was the real program for Sister Consolata's spiritual life, a program which she summed up in these words: "To truly love Thee, O Jesus, means to die rather than to permit one useless thought to enter, to die rather than to pronounce one sentence which has not been demanded or is really necessary, to die rather than to interrupt the act of love!"

She was utterly sincere in what she said and wrote.

PURITY OF LOVE IN THE ACT OF LOVE

In the preceding paragraphs it has been shown that the unceasing act of love cannot be carried out unless the soul maintains a rigorous silence of thought and word. Now we must add that the unceasing act of love is in turn a very great aid, in fact for the greater number of souls it is indispensible, in maintaining the virginal purity of mind and not permitting it to wander; it is the same with the heart by not letting it dwell upon anything earthly; and therefore, also the same with speech, by keeping the soul in a continual, virtuous silence. On this point also, the divine instructions to Sister Consolata are very clear. Jesus told her on September 16th, 1936, concerning the purity of mind and speech:

It is necessary for you to have such a mastery over your thoughts and over your speech that the devil can achieve nothing against you any more; such a mastery is facilitated by the act of love.

Concerning the purity of heart He told her on December 1st, 1935:

Only the continuity of the act of love can insure the virginal purity of your heart.

To that end Jesus not only demanded of Sister Consolata the continuity of the act of love, but even the virginal purity of the act of love; she was not to lose one heartfelt act of love throughout the day, and even more: she was never to take her mind off it.

This is true and perfect virginal purity of love!

As early as October 17th, 1935, Jesus had put her on her guard against the plotting of the enemy concerning the continuity of her act of love:

Take notice! What the enemy wants to keep you from, is the continual act of love. That is the reason for all this assailing struggle of thoughts. Any thought satisfies him, even a good one, so long as it keeps you from loving Me!

Then, on December 6th, 1935, He explained more clearly in what virginal purity of love consists:

Do you know in what the purity of your act of love consists? In not intermingling with it one other single thought; for it is possible for you to be loving with the heart and yet be thinking of something else with the mind at the same time. The purity of the act of love excludes every other thought and requires a virginal purity of mind. Do you understand? That is how I desire the act of love from you. But have no fear, I will assist you to offer it in all its purity. And so, by not permitting anything else to enter, you give Me, by loving, everything!

And He explained further how thoughts which are not related to love can mar the purity of the act of love:

You see, even in good thoughts which creep in, there is always a bit of self-love, of complacency; and it is easy to see how they will spoil the act of love. But if you will have complete trust in Me, that I am attending to everything and will continue to do so, and if you will not permit even one other thought to enter, then your act of love will possess a virginal purity.

When Sister Consolata made a formal promise that she wished to be faithful in maintaining the purity of her act of love, Jesus encouraged her with these words:

You promise Me virginal purity in love, and I promise you in turn its scrupulous observance. (December 8th, 1935)

Jesus later confirmed her through grace in the continuity and purity of her love, but not even so singular a favor brought her freedom from struggle or dispensed her from employing every possible spiritual force:

If I confirm you through grace in the virginal purity of love, you must not think that it will cost you no further effort to love Me. Oh no! Confirming you in grace does not preclude struggle and effort! (December 15th, 1935)

Now, to struggle means to suffer, and for Sister Consolata this meant continual suffering since the struggle also was continuous. But how precious is the fruit of pure love: purity of suffering! The soul who is thus established in an unceasing act of pure love is able to make all the fragrance of her suffering ascend to God without dissipating it in sterile laments or in a dangerous falling back upon herself, and that without striking an external pose as of a victim; none of those studied or willed attitudes which are attributed to victim-souls in fiction, are theirs in reality! Jesus confirmed all this when He said on December 9th, 1935:

You see, virginal purity of love parallels virginity of mind. When a soul establishes herself in this virginity of love, nothing can succeed in disturbing her any further; she will be confirmed in peace as it were.

Behold the Blessed Virgin at the foot of the Cross. She suffers, yes; but what dignity in her suffering! Can you see her? . . . In a sea of anguish, not one lament! She does not become despondent or discouraged; nothing of the kind! . . . She accepts and suffers; she offers it all up with calmness and strength, even to the 'consummatum est.' That is the way I wish you to be in the days of sorrow; the virginal purity of your love will help you to be so!

On December 10th, 1935: Jesus gave her the reason why purity of love establishes a soul in so perfect and stable a peace:

Amen, amen, I say to you: that whosoever committeth sin, is the servant of sin.[2] *And so with you, if you permit one thought to enter, if you pronounce one sentence that is not in reply to a question, then you will remain a slave to your infidelity. The servant is a slave, and slavery weighs heavily. Just so, after an infidelity you feel your soul enveloped by sadness, and you do not know how to rise again, except by having recourse to Jesus. Conversely, if you resist the temptation and are faithful, then you feel yourself free and strong and ready for all manner of suffering. Do you understand, Consolata? Remember this!*

Together with strength in suffering, virginal purity of love assures to the soul true joy which no one and nothing can take from her. She is as it were confirmed in joy, as she is in peace:

Consolata, look at the whiteness of the snow all about you. . . Just so must you remain in virginal purity of mind, of speech, and of heart; then suffering will always be sweet to you. For only unfaithfulness makes you suffer, nothing else! To suffer for the love of Jesus and of souls, is a joy! (December 13th, 1935)

---

2. John 8:34.

Our Lord's reminder of the whiteness of the snow expresses very well another fruit of the purity of love, which is that it brings the soul to an extreme purity, especially of mind:

You see, while you are loving Me, the enemy cannot enter with a single bad thought because all your faculties are absorbed in loving. But if you cease to love, he can do so very well. So you must always love! (December 2nd, 1935)

The same is true of purity of soul and body:

This unceasing act of love procures for you the triple virginity of the heart, the body, and the spirit. (June 11th, 1936)

That is so because, faithful to His promises, Jesus communicates His own virginal purity to the soul that is so intimately united with Him:

Consolata, virginal purity of mind: yes, in Me alone! . . . Virginity of heart: yes, in Me alone! . . . Purity of suffering: for Me alone! . . . Purity of speech: speak only with Me! . . . virginity of the heart, the body, and the spirit. (November 25th, 1935)

In truth, how great must be the purity of a soul who, from morning to night, unceasingly holds all her faculties riveted on one continuous and virginal act of love! What Jesus told Sister Consolata on November 30th, 1935 holds true for all souls:

Virginal purity of mind renders you beautiful and immaculate. The continuous act of love makes you fervent the way I desire you to be!

With these lessons on the purity of love Jesus was preparing Sister Consolata for her vow of virginal, pure love. We quote from her diary on August 6th, 1936:

". . . I have come to understand this: Jesus thirsts for love. Now, to quench that thirst with impure water would be an outrage which the heart of a bride cannot permit; therefore, my act of love which is to quench the thirst of Jesus, must attain such purity as not to allow any admixture of alien thoughts, even good ones; nothing, absolutely nothing will I let enter! My one and only preoccupation shall be to think of Jesus. . . He has given me to understand that during these days He has been preparing me for the vow of unceasing, virginal love which excludes every other thought, even a good one, and every sentence which is not strictly necessary. I have understood it to be His will that I should offer this vow this evening; I have placed it in His Sacred Heart. When He asked me what I desired in exchange, I replied: 'Fidelity to observe this vow until death.' It was made clear to me that He was assuming this responsibility for making me observe it."

As may be readily seen, it was a case of two vows of unheard-of difficulty and of the highest perfection. To simplify matters, her spiritual director later united the preceding vows into a single one which embraced all the others: the vow of the unceasing act of virginal love. She had to concentrate all her efforts not only on the continuity of the act of love but upon its virginal purity, and that without ever relaxing her complete self-surrender at any time of the day. That meant indeed being a victim of love! She wrote on January 1st, 1936:

"What Jesus is to me, that I also want to be to Him: a little victim, radiating immaculate purity of mind, tongue and heart."

That she had indeed become one, was assured her by Jesus on July 19th, 1936:

You are now a victim, consecrated to Love through Infinite Love!

INTENSITY OF LOVE IN THE ACT OF LOVE

This is the third requirement for perfect love, to give it the greatest possible intensity. "Thou shalt love the Lord thy God . . . with thy whole strength."[3] If we ought to love our neighbor as Jesus loved us, how much more ought we to love Jesus in order to reciprocate His love! Saint Bernard teaches that the only measure of our love of God is to love Him beyond measure. That wish to love Jesus "as no one has ever loved Him" is found in every saint, and it ought also to be found in every soul, at least by desire and endeavor.

Jesus loved Sister Consolata with an intense predilection, and this she returned with a most ardent love. We cannot enumerate here all the extraordinary graces and sublime gifts which Jesus bestowed upon her, but will limit ourselves to a few short quotations which relate most closely to the unceasing act of love. He told her on November 10th, 1936:

Consolata, henceforth we must not merely strive to avoid defects, but our efforts must aim at loving Jesus even to the extremes of folly! I wish to be ardently loved by you!

Can a soul arrive at that? Yes, with the grace of God; and by what means does one arrive at so intense a love? By the unceasing act of love. On July 22nd, 1936, Jesus made Sister Consolata feel His pressing invitation:

Love Me, Consolata, Love Me deeply!

---

3. Mark 12:30.

And when she inquired how she could come to love Him deeply, He replied:

Through the unceasing act of love one comes to love Me deeply!

And a few days later, on August 2nd:

Through the unceasing act of love you will love Me ardently!

Everything tends to add intensity to this continual act of love. In fact, the Blessed Virgin so instructed Sister Consolata, as we may judge from an entry in her diary, dated July 14th, 1936:

"... During recreation it had been stated that she loves Jesus most who makes the most sacrifices. While pondering over these words during this evening's meditation, I became saddened because I do not make any great sacrifices for Jesus, and yet I have so intense a desire to love Him ardently! Am I not, therefore, a poor deluded being? ... I raised my eyes to the statue of the Blessed Virgin in front of me, and as I regarded it, a comforting thought shot through me: what great thing had Our Lady done during her earthly sojourn at Nazareth? And yet no creature will ever surpass her in her love of God. While I was thinking of her and promising to imitate her, I heard these words: 'In order to love Jesus deeply, you must do everything possible to make your unceasing act of love as intense as possible.'"

From the fact that God Himself had to intervene and moderate Sister Consolata's loving impetuousness, it may be inferred that she actually did love as intensely as is humanly possible through her unceasing act of love. God the Father told her on November 29th, 1935:

Remain calm also in your act of love. For if you do not proceed with calmness but force your heart, the latter will become exhausted and will not be able to continue with its song! You must not think that it is less intense when it is more calm! Calmness insures its continuity, do you understand? Love is a fire in itself. Permit it to consume quietly My little victim! Love in peace. Let love consume you softly, not with fury and vehemence, for that would merely exhaust you and keep you from delighting Me with your song!

Jesus exhorted her in the same sense on another occasion. She was using the sewing machine, and since it was her intention to have every stitch an act of love, she tried to make the machine work very fast so as to perform more acts of love. However, she was soon forced to stop, for in her haste she had sewed the hem crookedly. Thereupon Jesus inspired her to proceed with calmness and drew a lesson from the incident:

You see, Consolata, it is the same with your act of love. If you continue to love Me with calmness, you will be able to offer Me this unceasing act of love. On the other hand, if you force your heart to love Me impetuously, you will be obliged to stop, for you will lack the strength to continue.

We would have to reproduce the greater part of her letters and the most fervent notations in her diary in order to portray the ardor of love which gradually grew up in the heart of this generous victim through the unceasing act of love. It is a fact that her poor heart, being too small to contain such a conflagration of love, suffered physically from it. On July 4th, 1936, she wrote:

"This evening I was able to remain for a little while before the blessed tabernacle. (My poor heart is beginning to be consumed and cannot contain all the desires and outbursts of love.) I felt myself pervaded by an infinite urge to love

Jesus, who loves me ardently, with a love of equal ardor: and as I repeated to Jesus the infinite desire to love Him, I felt within my heart another heart: the Sacred Heart! That was able to launch Itself into the Infinite without destroying nature!"

LOVE OF ABANDONMENT AND THE UNCEASING ACT OF LOVE

This is the highest expression of the life of love and the logical corollary of what has been said so far. The act of love ought to be so unceasing that not one act would be willingly lost throughout the day; it ought to be so virginally pure that no other thought could enter. To attain this, it is necessary for the soul to carry her faith in Love so high as to abandon herself to Love like a feather to the breeze. In other words, it is necessary to abandon herself so irrevocably to Love as to renounce not only every thought of other creatures, but even every thought of herself. It means to obliterate herself, to die to herself—a difficult matter, and one which is little understood by the majority of souls—but it is, therefore, no less necessary if Jesus is to have freedom of action within the soul.

When speaking of the life of love in general, we already pointed out that to forget oneself and to abandon oneself to God does not imply that the soul should neglect her own spiritual development and relax into blameworthy indifference; the soul should avoid proceeding according to her own whims and preferences; instead, she should comply with the workings of Jesus in the soul with simplicity and docility. Our Lord's watchword to all souls whom He calls to high perfection in the path of love is simply this: *Allow Me to do it!*

Yes, let Jesus do it! And why not? Has anyone else the sanctification of the soul more at heart than He? Is anyone else able to sanctify her? Who can perceive her real needs as well as He? To Him alone are known the designs which God has for the soul. Being omnipotent, He can do everything; being faithfulness itself, He will keep all His promises! . . . Why then should one not entrust oneself to Him and give Him a free hand so that He can work in the soul as absolute and uncontested Master? Why not submit to Him one's own opinions, one's thoughts, aspirations, desires, preoccupations? Why not adapt oneself trustingly at each moment to His actions which alone are always sanctifying? That is what Jesus desired from Sister Consolata on September 22nd, 1935:

You see, Consolata, sanctity means self-forgetfulness in everything, in thoughts, desires, words. . . Allow Me to do it all! I will do everything; but you should, at every moment, give Me what I ask for with much love!

Love of abandonment, therefore, resolves itself in practice into docile love. In speaking to the multitude, Jesus reminded them that it was written by the Prophet: "They shall all be taught of God."[4] Jesus is the sole teacher of all souls: "Neither be ye called masters; for one is your Master, Christ."[5] He is the Master who possesses the knowledge of sanctity in an infinite degree, and He wants to and is able to communicate it to the soul. But the soul must lend herself to being instructed and must execute with promptness

---

4. Isaias 54:13; John 6:45.
5. Matthew 23:10.

every divine command or wish, no matter whether it be pleasing or painful, and without regard to the manner in which it is manifested. Thus, Jesus told Sister Consolata on September 24th, 1935:

Consolata, I have every claim upon you, but you have only one duty: to obey Me. I require a docile will which permits Me to act, which lends itself to everything, which trusts in Me and serves Me always in peace and joy, no matter what the situation is.

Jesus is God, and whatever He does, He does as God, that is, He does everything divinely well and for the greatest benefit of the soul, even though the soul does not always perceive within herself the divine workings and their results:

Let Me do everything! You will see that I will do everything, and do it well, and that My little victim will become fruitful in love and in souls! (November 18th, 1935)

It is love, and love only, that can bring the soul to this complete and trusting abandonment. For how could the soul renounce every thought, desire, and personal preoccupation, if she did not entrust herself to Love and permit all thoughts, desires, and preoccupations to become absorbed in love? If Jesus is ready to do everything Himself in the soul, He does so precisely in order that the soul may concentrate upon loving Him. This He confirmed to Sister Consolata on November 8th, 1935:

I delight to work in a soul. You see, I love to do everything Myself; and from this soul I ask only that she love Me.

Many souls fall into the error of believing that they can sanctify themselves; they want to do it themselves, instead of leaving it to Jesus; they wish to select the path, the means; in short, they wish to instruct the Master. He is the true sanctifier. A soul is more quickly and completely sanctified by

Him, the more she has succeeded in eliminating the encumbrance of herself on the path to holiness, and the more she shows herself docile to the touch of the divine Master, for that is characteristic of how the gifts of the Holy Spirit work. From this it becomes easy to understand correctly the words which Jesus addressed to Sister Consolata on August 22nd, 1934:

Think no longer about yourself, about your perfection, on how to attain to sanctity, or about your defects, your present and future troubles. No. I will see to your sanctification, to your sanctity. You must henceforth think only of Me and of souls; of Me to love Me, and of souls to save them!

And that is precisely what she did by means of the unceasing virginal act of love: love and souls; nothing else. The unceasing act of love is, therefore, not only a most efficacious means for perfecting love in that it is continual, pure, and intense, but it is also a sublime means for arriving at the perfect love of abandonment. Jesus told Sister Consolata on October 15th, 1935:

Let Me do everything! Act as though only I existed. Of yourself there should remain only the continual act of love and an extreme docility to do simply and always whatever I desire directly or indirectly through your superior or your Sisters.

When a soul renounces herself and her every thought in order to offer to Jesus an unceasing and virginal pure act of love, Jesus takes upon Himself the care of that soul. And His solicitude is more loving than an earthly mother's when she presses her offspring to her heart in an effusion of love:

Follow Me with an unceasing act of love, day by day,

hour by hour, minute by minute! I will attend to everything else! I will provide for everything! (May 21st, 1936)

Sister Consolata exhibited a marvelous activity. Her ambition was, throughout each day, to place herself at the service of all. She did not lack work; she was secretary, cook, porter, shoemaker, and was always ready to be of assistance to anyone. Now and then it happened that she became uneasy lest so many different duties might keep her from doing justice to everything, but on one such occasion Jesus admonished her:

Let everything else in you be silent. Only: 'Jesus, Mary, I love You! Save souls!' And rest assured that I am thinking of everything and making every provision, even to finding the time for repairing the sandals. You see, it is the devil who is trying to overwhelm you with work and cause you anxiety about all the various demands made upon you simultaneously. No, I am thinking of everything, and I will also let you find the necessary time for everything! (September 8th, 1936)

During her last years she had a presentiment of her approaching death, and it was only natural that she would ponder over the circumstances which would surround it. But on March 21st, 1942, Jesus told her:

Live a life of complete abandonment in God! As for the day, the hour, and the minute of your death, Jesus, the Blessed Virgin and Saint Joseph are thinking of that and preparing for it. You should concentrate solely upon loving Me and on saving souls!

We know from Our Lord's words which we have already quoted (October 8th, 1935), that Sister Consolata achieved a high degree of abandonment to Love through her unceasing virginal act of love:

Consolata, I am pleased with you because I am able to do all I wish, and it is I Who am working within you!

We can also learn it from her notes. We will quote here a few of her thoughts and resolutions which confirm and illustrate this important fact and put into clear relief the interior docility of this soul toward the workings of grace.

"I must forget myself; I must never think or be preoccupied about myself, nor ever demand that others should think of me. Jesus will take care of everything."

"To die and not to exist any more! If I think about myself, if I have even a good thought or preoccupation, if I speak about myself even in indifferent matters, that does not mean to die but to preserve life within me. And all that shows a lack of confidence in Jesus, as though He would not think or provide for Consolata down to the very smallest detail!"

"I must remember that, by the merciful choice of God, I am a victim of love. Now, a victim is a being which has been set apart. Jesus has sacrificed everything and has left me nothing but the wound in His Side and the unceasing act of love. . . The victim must be dead to everything and to herself; she must have but one occupation and one preoccupation: solely and always to love. Toward everything else, oblivion and indifference. O Jesus, grant that I may live this life like a true victim of love, that I may love this state and be generous, denying Thee nothing, no thought, no word, no act of virginal love. O Jesus, I place my trust in Thee!"

"Divinely illumined, I was given to understand that Jesus longed to have me carry my trust to extremes; in short, to abandon my soul completely and not to give her any further thought. Is it possible that God could not suffice for

Consolata? Could Consolata not place her trust so completely in God as to abandon her own soul entirely to Him without further thought or preoccupation? . . . Yes, I must let Him act and live within me without giving a thought to time or anything else; nothing, nothing, solely and always I must sing that I love Him, as though I did not exist any more and in the place of Consolata there existed solely this act of unceasing love!"

Sister Consolata bound herself to this life of perfect abandonment by the will of God and with the consent of her spiritual director on the feast of the Sacred Heart in 1937, using the following formula:

"O Sacred Heart of Jesus, through the heart of our heavenly Mother, I offer a vow of complete abandonment to Thee, to Thy will, in the certainty that Thou wilt think of everything, even to the minutest details. And I promise Thee complete self-effacement (thoughts, desires, etc.), to attend solely to offering Thee the unceasing act of virginal love, to see Thee in everything, and to have always a 'yes' ready for everything. O Jesus, I place my trust in Thee!"

Sister Consolata's heroic fidelity to this vow procured for her a profound and unshakable spiritual peace, even in her incessant struggle:

"I can no longer ask anything else from Jesus but that His holy will be accomplished. I feel myself so indifferent, so extraneous to everything, that I dare compare myself to a babe, sleeping on the Sacred Heart. Since the day when I abandoned myself to Him and begged Him please to take complete charge of Consolata, I have been enjoying an enviable peace and experiencing a constant joy. Jesus thinks of everything, of absolutely everything, so that I have nothing more to wish for. At present, the life of abandonment even removes the pain of discouragement when I realize that I am giving God nothing, absolutely nothing!"

In reality she was giving everything with her unceasing and virginal act of love, with her "yes" to everything and everybody.

In this perfect abandonment to Love, in this incessant craving for the salvation of souls, Sister Consolata lived, labored, and died. Even on her death-bed, while her body was racked with pain and her spirit groaned in the anxieties of utter darkness, this generous victim-soul never interrupted her canticle of virginal love. With her last breath, her "Jesus, Mary, I love You! Save souls!" reached heaven and perpetuated itself there in conformity with what Jesus had promised her:

Your act of love will not cease with your death but will continue to all eternity in heaven! (November 7th, 1935)

- VI -

THE UNCEASING ACT OF LOVE IN THE SPIRITUAL LIFE OF SISTER CONSOLATA

THE ACT OF LOVE AND VOCAL PRAYER

WE have already explained what love means in the life of the soul. Now let us examine more closely a few points about the unceasing act of love itself.

Above all, what can be said about the unceasing act of love in relation to the many and varied vocal prayers? Sister Consolata was a prayerful soul. In her writings she speaks again and again of her soul's immense need to become and remain absorbed in prayer. Her life is a practical example of how a soul can put into practice the Gospel precept: "We ought always to pray, and not to faint."[1] Her sanctity is a concrete proof of the omnipotence of humble, trusting, and constant prayer. The First Fridays of each month, for example, were her great feast days, for then she was permitted

---

1. Luke 18:1.

to pass as much as eight hours in adoration before Jesus solemnly exposed in the Blessed Sacrament. Jesus Himself had told her on March 31st, 1934:

Prayer shall be your fortress!

For this reason she clung ardently to the community exercises of piety, and this also from a love of regularity, observance, and good example. She had well understood and taken to heart the admonition which Jesus had given her one day:

Everything that distracts you from pious practices such as Holy Mass, Communion, the Divine Office, meditation, is not good, and proceeds not from Me!

But outside of these pious exercises which were made in common, and the Way of the Cross, which she made every morning upon arriving early in choir, and sometimes also in her cell in the evening, she practiced no other, or hardly any. Vocal prayer was for her spirit almost a torment. Her soul stood in need of one thing only: love. And in the unceasing act of love she found what is contained in other prayer forms. Jesus too reminds us: "When you are praying, speak not much, as the heathens. For they think that in their much speaking they may be heard."[2] Sister Consolata once wrote to her spiritual director:

". . . The Gospel passage 'He that eateth My Flesh, and drinketh My Blood, abideth in Me, . . . and shall live by Me'[3] brings me joy beyond measure, for it gives me the sweet certainty that by my act of love I am living and throbbing in the Sacred Heart and that I will live there eternally. I feel that I am living in Him, and that this act of love attaches

---

2. Matthew 6:7.
3. John 6:57-58.

me eternally to Him, soaring high above everything, above myself and everything that surrounds me. But the joy that derives from this intimacy is often disturbed by vocal prayers. Then my poor soul is shot through with distractions. . . As you see, Father, love has simplified everything; even a soul who is extremely active, enjoys complete repose by means of her unceasing act of love."

As Saint Thomas puts it: "The soul really and fully lives her life when she carries out the divine intentions in her regard."[4]

Sister Consolata's personal experience is that of every soul who has attained a high degree of unitive love. So it is not to be wondered at that she resolved: "I must not interrupt the act of love in order to formulate prayers. Jesus knows all my intentions!" Was she mistaken or correct in this? The divine teaching tells us that she was pursuing the right path; for, being fearful one day that her inability to formulate prayers was caused by laziness, she complained:

"O Jesus, I do not know how to pray!"

Our Lord calmed her by saying:

Tell Me, what more beautiful prayer do you want to offer Me? 'Jesus, Mary, I love You! Save souls!' Love and souls! What more beautiful prayer could you desire? (October 6th, 1935)

Mother Abbess, having noticed how Sister Consolata spent herself in work to the detriment of her health, once considered it opportune to dispense her from certain duties so as to afford her more time for prayer. The good Sister wished to obey, but felt incapable of praying more vocal

---

4. I, 16, 4, ad. 3.

prayers and so hastened to the feet of the divine Master: "O Jesus, teach me to pray!" This was His reply:

You think you do not know how to pray?... What prayer is more beautiful and more acceptable to Me than the act of love? Do you know what Jesus is doing in the tabernacle? He is loving the Father and He is loving souls. That is all. No sound of words, nothing. Only silence and love. So, do the same! No, my dear, do not add any prayers; no, no, no! Gaze upon the tabernacle, and love in that way! (November 17th, 1935)

Jesus referred again on December 12th, 1935 to vocal prayers in addition to those prescribed by the rule:

I prefer one of your acts of love to all your prayers!

He also explained—and this is important and comforting to all who will be following Sister Consolata in that same path—that the invocation on behalf of souls, as contained in the formula of the unceasing act of love, extends to all souls:

'Jesus, Mary, I love You! Save souls!' This comprises all: the souls in purgatory and those in the Church Militant, the innocent and the sinful souls, the dying, the Godless, etc. (June 20th, 1940)

Let us repeat once more that the practice of the unceasing act of love does not in any way prejudice the prayers prescribed by the rule or those particular prayers to which a soul feels herself drawn. Grace should not be anticipated, but followed. Grace will suggest to the soul when it is opportune to substitute the unceasing act of love for this or that free prayer.

THE ACT OF LOVE AND MEDITATION

Sister Consolata was always faithful in observing community meditation and mental prayer. But she never succeeded in meditating according to any fixed method; this is, after all, also the case with other souls who incline by preference to the prayer of simplicity. "Young bees," writes Saint Francis de Sales, "are called grubs until they are able to make honey. Similarly, prayer is called meditation until it has produced the honey of devotion. Then it becomes contemplation. The longing for divine love makes us meditate; but once won, love causes us to contemplate."[5]

Sister Consolata had attained precisely this affectionate and unceasing union with God, so it is understandable that everything which books could say left her for the most part indifferent, and sometimes was more of a hindrance than a help. She writes:

". . . The vine branch does not produce grapes by itself, but only when it is attached to the trunk of the vine. Now this union with the trunk (Jesus) is favored by the unceasing act of love. Now Jesus no longer requires lengthy meditations and reading from me. For my soul they would be a waste of time. The important thing for me is to yield much fruit, that is to love much, to love unceasingly."

Jesus taught her in the same sense when she inquired of Him one day why she was unable to meditate or derive light, nourishment, and fervor from the beautiful books which were being read aloud; He explained that the same food

---

5. *Of the Love of God*, Book 6, chapter 3.

was not suitable for every constitution, that a delicate stomach is unable to digest ordinary food which is beneficial to a robust one, and that to her He had assigned the Gospel. Certainly, the spiritual food of which a beginner stands in need is different from that of a proficient soul or one who has already arrived at the unitive life.

After a certain meditation on the end of man, Sister Consolata was racking her brain on how to direct her life intentions, when Jesus told her (September 1935):

You are too little to form intentions. I will decide the purpose of your life. Just love Me continually, and do not interrupt your act of love!

Still another time, and again in order to calm her concerning her inability to meditate, Jesus told her:

It is no longer the hour to meditate or to read, but now is the time to love Me, to behold Me and see Me in everyone, to suffer with joy and with thanksgiving! (April 3rd, 1936)

No matter what the theme of the meditation, the divine Voice and Light always recalled her spirit to the exercise of the unceasing act of love. One day she had been unable to hear the point of the meditation and sought to substitute the Gospel. On opening the book, she read: "Prepare ye the way of the Lord. . . Every valley shall be filled, and every mountain and hill shall be brought low; and the crooked ways shall be made straight and the rough ways plain."[6] The meditation period was almost ended when Jesus gave her to understand:

The act of love does all this in a soul: it fills every void and lays low all pride. (October 10th, 1935)

Again, on July 25th, 1936, when the meditation was on

---

6. Luke 3:4-6.

the Gospel passage; "Watch ye and pray."[7] Jesus told her: *'Do not worry! I am watching in you; I am praying in you. It is for you to love Me, and only that!'*

As one can see, everything was to bring her, and everything did in fact bring her, to the unceasing act of love. After a meditation on the prodigal son, she noted in her diary:

"Yes, Jesus gave me the most beautiful gown: love. He placed on my finger the ring of fidelity, and on my feet the sandals of confidence. And in return the Good God asks only for the unceasing act of love."

And after a meditation on Our Lord's words to Saint Peter: "Couldst thou not watch one hour?"[8] she wrote:

"I must remember this divine saying throughout the day in order to give to Jesus entire hours of love."

And again on August 20th, 1936:

"During meditation I understood that my act of love is like the treasure hidden in the field, and like the pearl described in the Gospel parable; in order to possess this treasure I must sell all. What remained to me still to sell? A few sentences which escaped me during recreation. I determined to be more faithful. I willed it and I kept my promise. After the victory I found myself much stronger in the exercise of virtue."

It was not, therefore, a case of her neglecting or failing to attribute sufficient importance to meditation. On the contrary. But for her, meditation did not mean an exercise of the mind, but a tranquil repose of her heart in love: to love, to love unceasingly, to remove every obstacle that impeded the perfect continuity and purity of love.

---

7. Matthew 26:41.
8. Mark 14:37.

All this, we believe, will be of comfort and assistance to souls, particularly to those who have already progressed in the unitive life and who are experiencing the same difficulty with a multiplicity of vocal prayers and with methodical meditation; and also to all souls without exception on the days when the spirit is unable to concentrate on a point of reflection for reasons of aridity and so on. What is to be done then? Rack one's brain in order to extract even one good thought? It would be a loss of time. Let the mind wander? No. Instead, the soul can always love; and every act of love, even when done with an effort of the will, has always great value for merit and sanctification. Saint Thomas also teaches that the continuity of our love makes up for our weakness in contemplation.[9]

THE ACT OF LOVE AND SPIRITUAL READING

As with meditation, so also is spiritual reading in general of the greatest usefulness to most souls.

Sister Consolata never omitted the reading required by her rule, but beyond that she read little or nothing. In general, she felt no need to seek enlightenment from books. Referring to her first years as a Capuchin nun, she writes:

"I have never read ascetical books, and I read no books now. Besides the rule, the constitution, and directives, I keep only the *Imitation of Christ* and the *Holy Gospels* ready at hand. For spiritual reading I use *The Story of a Soul*, and this suffices . . . for my whole life!"

Actually, it did not serve her for her entire life, for Jesus later made her put that away also.

---

9. II, II, 180, ad. 1.

Aside from the fact that Jesus instructed her directly, there applies here what we have already said in connection with meditation: the purpose of such books certainly is to bring the soul to love God and her neighbor in a spirit of sacrifice. Now the spiritual life of Sister Consolata was already practically one unceasing act of love, a "yes" to everything. What could books teach her that would be any better? She writes:

"A book or a page, no matter how beautiful, makes me interrupt the act of love. Jesus desires my love to be entire and uninterrupted."

She did not change her opinion even when the divine Voice became silent in her soul. One of her Sisters once loaned her a book entitled *With Jesus Alone*. Sister Consolata kept it for several months, then returned it secretly so as not to have to confess to not having read it:

". . . One day, in a period of darkness, I sought enlightenment in the book *With Jesus Alone*. I was soon overwhelmed with doubts and understood nothing any more. A good thing that my spiritual director put my little bark on even keel again. I have learned my lesson and I give up the one book which has remained to me. The *Holy Gospel* will be Consolata's food henceforth for the rest of her life."

During 1936 she noted in her diary:

"Before beginning the holy exercises I had noticed in the library a life of St. Gerard Majella. The desire to know this saint who turned every stitch into an act of love, made me put that book aside until I could obtain permission to use it for my spiritual reading during those holy days. But even before I could ask Mother Abbess, Jesus made Himself heard in my soul: why not rather read His book, the *Holy Gospel?* In the lives of the saints one needs to read entire chapters in order to find words of eternal life, but in His divine Book every word would be food for eternal life for me. I accepted this divine inspiration and did my spiritual reading in the Holy Gospel. Every passage brought me enlightenment and nourishment."

Sister Consolata never gave up that book of the Holy Gospel! During the dark hours of the spirit she had recourse to it and always found the light she needed. She writes:

"Jesus makes me understand the Holy Gospel very well. Upon opening it at random my glance often happens to fall on the words of Saint Elizabeth: 'Blessed art thou that hast believed!'[10] Consolata also desires to believe, oh so deeply, in the Good God!"

Yes, to believe in the Good God by offering Him an unceasing act of virginal love, that is the sense in which Jesus made her understand the Gospel:

"I have found so much light in the Gospel. 'He that abideth in Me, and I in him, the same beareth much fruit.'[11] My great desire to be fruitful is satisfied by it. Not only that, but by remaining in Jesus through the unceasing act of love, my prayer too will be heard, for it says in the Gospel: 'If you abide in Me, and My words abide in you, you shall ask whatever you will, and it shall be done unto you.'[12] O my God, Thou hast exceeded all my expectations! I need only to observe Thy commandments with fidelity in order to be certain of persevering in Thy love. And to obtain this: 'Jesus, Mary, I love You! Save souls!'"

---

10. Luke 1:45.
11. John 15:5.
12. John 15:7.

"In my mind I keep hearing the words of the Blessed Virgin at the wedding feast in Cana: 'Whatsoever He shall say to you, do ye!'[13] And because my spiritual director has told me never to deny Jesus one single act of love, I seek to do just that. This now comprises my entire life, and in carrying it out, life has become marvelously simple. Nothing else! No one else! In that way, virginal love can soar freely!"

"One passage in the Holy Gospel has given me particular confidence: 'All power is given to Me in heaven and on earth.'[14] 'O Jesus,' I said, 'use this Thy power in my soul and establish me in the unceasing act of love so that I may not lose one! Thou canst do it!' "

" 'He that is not with Me, is against Me; and he that gathereth not with Me, scattereth.'[15] When I am not with Jesus in a continuous act of love, I am against Him, I am scattering."

" 'If any man will come after Me, let him deny himself, and take up his cross, and follow Me.'[16] If I do not carry the cross of the unceasing act of love, I am not following Jesus, and therefore, I cannot follow Him to Calvary."

It is superfluous to point out that all these interpretations of the Gospel texts have no exegetical value; Sister Consolata simply adapted them to her own spiritual needs.

We have made particular mention of the Gospels, but Sister Consolata loved and delighted in all holy writings:

"I am ignorant in the extreme, and yet I often receive so much enlightenment during the recital of the Divine Office concerning the Latin words I pronounce, that I understand

---

13. John 2:5.
14. Matthew 28:18.
15. Luke 11:23.
16. Matthew 16:24.

and enjoy them more than if they were written in Italian."

". . . If Jesus is silent now, the Father in heaven nevertheless does not fail to provide directly the food for His little bird; He nourishes me with choice grains by letting me find them in Holy Scripture, in fact He Himself hands them out to me. And at Matins last night, my thought was arrested during the first lesson by: "Quis ergo nos separabit a caritate Christi? (Who then shall separate us from the love of Christ?)[17] No. In union with the Apostle I joyfully repeat that no creature can now separate me from my unceasing act of love."

What is here said concerning spiritual reading properly speaking, applies equally to the reading in the refectory. One day Sister Consolata's mind was struck by this passage: "Find for yourself some task that will completely absorb you." On entering these words in her notebook, she added this comment:

"What must completely absorb me, is a continuous 'Jesus, Mary, I love You! Save souls!'"

On May 9th, 1936, she writes:

"Yesterday's mealtime reading told of Our Lord's desire for wholehearted and perfect victim-souls, and this morning the divine Light explained to me that if I were to cut even a small part from a magnificent peach, it would no longer be presentable at the royal table. Just so, if my soul omits some acts of love through an extraneous thought or word, the victim will no longer be complete and perfect, and therefore, no longer presentable at the table of the Divine King."

---

17. Romans 8:35.

THE ACT OF LOVE AND THE PARTICULAR EXAMEN

Concerning the particular examen of one's conscience, that indispensable means for maintaining and increasing spiritual fervor, Sister Consolata wrote as follows:

". . . It is necessary for me to convince myself once and for all that to make a particular examen on any point other than the unceasing act of virginal love is for my soul only a waste of time and energy; it would mean leaving the road which God wants me to follow. Therefore, my particular examen shall solely and always be concerned with the unceasing act of love, the purity of mind. . . I have come to understand that it is better for me to concentrate all my energies on that, and not to dissipate them in numerous resolutions."

One sees, she had simplified her spiritual life also in this respect. This does not mean that she did not appreciate sufficiently the value of the particular examen; on the contrary, it occupied a place of first importance in her spiritual life. She did not in fact limit it to the few minutes required by her daily schedule, but in a sense she prolonged it throughout the entire day. Jesus had taught her to renew her resolution of the unceasing virginal act of love at every hour throughout the day, and to this she would add a rapid examen of the hour just passed.

To that end she would enter in a little notebook which she always carried with her for that purpose, any infidelities in the continuity or purity of her love. In that way she had before her in the evening, when she made a comprehensive examen of the entire day, the clear and precise state of her soul. She would then ask pardon and would make reparation for her infidelity by making crosses on the floor with her tongue or by kissing the crucifix. After that she would take up again, calmly and trustingly, her song of love.

We do not say that such a method would be suitable for every soul, nor even a majority of souls. But for Sister Consolata, who longed to respond fully to grace, it was a necessity. To offer an unceasing act of virginal love in fact requires of the soul an extreme vigilance over herself, and the act is really impossible without controlling and renewing one's fervor as often as possible.

On the other hand, to conduct the particular examen and concentrate always on one point, made its practice easier; and the divine promises concerning the unceasing act of love, which we have already mentioned, gave her the certainty that through it she would attain all the rest, that is, the perfection of every virtue.

THE ACT OF LOVE AND THE SPIRITUAL RETREAT

The days of the monthly retreat were always for Sister Consolata, so to speak, days of spiritual provisioning. She made her retreats, therefore, with scrupulous fidelity and diligence, and since each Capuchin nun was free to choose for herself the most suitable day, she selected the First Friday of each month.

She began her preparation on the preceding evening during the Holy Hour in choir from eleven to midnight. She writes:

"During the monthly day of recollection Jesus would

nourish and instruct my soul with some thought and engrave it upon my heart."

She also mentions some of these thoughts, as for instance: "The Son of Man is not come to be ministered unto, but to minister,"[18] or "He emptied Himself, taking the form of a servant."[19]

"What great enlightenment and resolutions!" she writes.

But here again, enlightenment and resolutions were always related to her particular vocation of love, that is, the unceasing act of love. At the close of the monthly retreat day or on the Sunday after, she would send a detailed report on the state of her soul to her spiritual director, as he had enjoined upon her and Jesus had approved. We quote in part from one such report, which was written after the First Friday in September 1942, four years before her death, when her health was already failing:

". . . Here I am, placing my poor soul at your feet, to receive in spirit your absolution and fatherly blessing, to gain new strength to carry on 'usque ad finem!'

"Your last letter has been my daily bread throughout the whole past month. I thank you for it from my heart! During August, it seems to me, love was more intense, although I must confess to the loss of two hours.[20] The unceasing effort to live the present moment helps me to center my attention on the unceasing act of love; it preserves my spirit in peace and frees it from all preoccupation over the morrow and what work to follow. On two occasions I indulged in

---

18. Matthew 20:28.
19. Philippians 2:7.
20. Sister Consolata's day of unceasing love counted 17 hours. To have lost two hours in a month is not much. Nevertheless, it must be pointed out that these omissions were not voluntary, but caused mostly by exterior circumstances of work, etc. . .

useless thoughts, five times in useless talk, twice I did not suffer gladly. My charity, it seems to me, is in order. If a reproof escapes me or I resent some words, etc., I immediately ask forgiveness without a thought for myself, so that peace might always reign in every heart around me.

"In the kitchen my struggle for self-denial continues, but now everything passes between Jesus and Consolata, 'to tell Thee that I love Thee!'

"During these days I have great need to pray in order to maintain myself on the heights. I feel tired... Obtain for me a little generosity so that I may defeat my selfish nature and launch myself generously on the road of daily sacrifice..."

THE ACT OF LOVE IN VARIOUS SPIRITUAL STATES

It is clear from what has already been said that the unceasing act of love was in truth the whole life of Sister Consolata, as indeed her whole life was one unceasing act of love. This was the case because she relied on the divine teaching and had faith in the act of love and its value. This value was above all intrinsic:

"I cannot communicate continuously, as is my need, but I have come to understand that an act of love brings Jesus into the soul, that is, it increases grace and is like a Communion."

She also knew its worth in regard to her own vocation and mission:

"The will of God, my vocation to attain to sanctity, is one continuous 'Jesus, Mary, I love You! Save souls!'... Every effort, every force and activity of the soul must be aimed at not interrupting the act of love. Nothing else; this alone! For that is my way, the way which Jesus has pointed out to me."

The act of love also has value because it eliminates from the spiritual life of so many Marthas the "turbaris erga plurima" (thou are troubled about many things).[21]

"Spiritually, Jesus demanded of me an absolute silence of thoughts and words, and of the heart an unceasing 'Jesus, Mary, I love You! Save souls!' The more faithful I am to this little way of love, the more is my soul flooded with joy and a true peace that nothing is able to disturb, not even my continual falls. For, when I bring these to Jesus, He makes me remedy them through acts of humility, and these in turn increase the peace and joy in my heart."

Finally, there remains the act's value for eternal life:

"How happy, active, and vigilant ought the certainty make me that my every act of love endures to all eternity!"

So there results one single, constant, and trusting prayer:

"O Jesus, grant that I may live entirely concealed in Thee, in complete self-effacement, so that Thou mayest always do what Thou wilt with me. Thou alone must remain, and an unceasing 'Jesus, Mary, I love You! Save souls!' Grant that of the seventeen hours in my day I may not lose one!

We might also add that the act of love was her one and only weapon against the enemy. For one cannot assume that the devil would leave this saintly soul in peace and let her act of love go unpunished. Hers was a battle without respite, carried on now and then in the open, but she came out victorious from every encounter by means of the act of love.

"The invincible weapon which always assures one the

---

21. Luke 10:41.

victory, is the unceasing act of love... (It) prepares the soul for the temptation, and it sustains it during the temptation; for love is everything! ... Therefore, I must not let myself become discouraged by the enemy; the act of love must dominate the struggle, never must the struggle dominate the act of love."

We must not think that Sister Consolata spoke and acted in this manner only on the days in which she walked in the light of divine favor. No. She did so also when she found herself in spiritual darkness, walking in the simple path of faith:

"It was nine o'clock in the evening when I came out of the sacristy and found myself in complete darkness on the upper stair landing. It was a bit hazardous to descend, but I clung to the railing, and by following it, calmly reached the bottom step. As I was descending I thought of how similar was the case of my own soul; complete darkness. But by clinging to the unceasing act of love, I will calmly arrive at my last hour... Yes, the act of love is really everything; it gives light and strength to proceed. Woe to my soul if she did not have this anchor of salvation to which to cling at certain times! I cannot fathom the abyss of despair into which I would fall!"

As in the days of aridity, so in the days of suffering. Well did she experience it, for to her the heights of love were never separated from those of suffering; and yet she could bear witness:

"The unceasing act of love keeps the soul always in peace. I believe that it has a strong ascendency over suffering and helps one to suffer joyfully... The act of love is stronger than any pain... I feel that the unceasing act of love maintains, and will continue to maintain, my little bark steady through all confusion, boredom and tediousness."

Sister Consolata did not, therefore, achieve continuity of love without a great effort or in a short space of time. Herein lies her merit, that she persevered in spite of everything, began each day anew, and corrected herself after every fall. And this through years and years, with heroic constancy and humble prayer. She left no means untried, and let no occasion pass for renewing her resolution. "The sluggard willeth and willeth not."[22] Sister Consolata was certainly not a sluggish soul, nor did she deceive herself with mere wishing. She willed seriously and strongly. Her energetic determination, as we have said, was one of the most outstanding characteristics of her spirit. The same impetuous character that had earned for her the nickname of "thunder and lightning," also directed and sustained her will in the good cause. All who knew her closely, admired her strong and firm will for good. That was due above all to her unceasing act of love. Her "I will" is to be found in her every resolution and is always entirely sincere. This fact is evident on every page of her writings:

"I wish to respond fully to divine grace and let this act fill my entire day from the first to the last Sign of the Cross. I wish my every act, however insignificant, to be performed with oh so much love! . . . No thunderstorm or stroke of lightning shall interrupt one continuous 'Jesus, Mary, I love You! Save souls!' . . . To see and treat Thee in everything. . . O Jesus, with Thine aid I will not deprive Thee of one act of love, not one! Yes, Jesus, that I will to do! And in order that I may keep faith with this 'I will,' I submerge it and leave it forever in Thy Most Precious Blood!"

---

22. Proverbs 13:4.

THE HEIGHT OF HEROISM IN THE UNCEASING ACT OF LOVE

It was always the same: effort and good will! Her iron will surmounted every trial, every renunciation, every sacrifice with firmness. She abhorred mediocrity, despised compromises, she had a heroic desire to reach the peak; and her heroism was continuous, as one may judge from the following words which she addressed to her spiritual director on August 28th, 1938; these might be termed her spiritual testament to all souls who wish to follow her:

"... Father, at present I feel an infinite desire within me to live 'the Littlest Way' even at the price of heroism.[23] I feel that I can do it if I really have the will! And so, I will it with all my strength, and I begin! Father, I sense an imperious duty to live my Littlest Way to the full. I wish I could call out to all the Littlest Souls throughout the world, when I am on the point of death: 'Follow me!' I will, indeed I will to offer the unceasing act of love from my awakening until I fall asleep, because Jesus has asked for it; and He has asked for it because I am able to give it to Him if I trust in Him alone!

"But my weakness is extreme, and temptations are not lacking. I need to rise up alone against them all and must continue by sheer will power. No, I do not wish to lead a cowardly existence, I wish to live heroically! I desire it with all the strength of my heart and of my will, and I wish to continue so until death. Jesus, who died on the Cross for love of me, merits it, and for love of Him I wish to live heroically!

---

23. That is, the way of the unceasing act of love. The origin and significance of such a terminology will be explained in the chapter which follows.

"But to live upon such heights does not please human nature and comes hard. I am in need of your prayers, Father, in order to persevere. On that peak alone do I find peace; there alone do I find joy and strength in suffering. If I live on these heights where there is only Christ Crucified, then I have need of continual sacrifice, as I do of the air I breathe.

"I see all this, I sense it, I understand it. That is why I do not feel right if I have not overcome every cowardice, even alone and in the face of all, and if I do not live my Littlest Way which I love so much! . . . O Father, pray that I may make my divine dream come true, else I shall be extremely unhappy! . . ."

These words reveal Sister Consolata completely, her soul and her life!

- VII -

A TANGIBLE FRUIT OF THE DIVINE MESSAGE: THE WORK OF THE LITTLEST ONES

JESUS REVEALS THE WORK OF THE LITTLEST ONES

THE work of the Littlest Ones represents the tangible fruit of this new manifestation of the Sacred Heart of Jesus, which is to grow and perpetuate itself throughout the world. The unceasing act of love, it is true, had to be the practical expression of Sister Consolata's life of love; but that still did not mean that she was supposed to pass it on to other souls. If we have, in the preceding pages, already used the terms "the Littlest Way of Love" and "the Littlest Ones," this was due only to the exigencies of the compilation. In reality Sister Consolata spoke solely of "the Little Way" and "the Little Souls" until the time when Jesus revealed to her the work of the "Littlest Ones."

In paging through her writings one perceives that she had no idea, at least in the beginning, that she was to show to the world a new spiritual way or to give life to a new work. The unceasing act of love seemed to her the means for realizing her own mission on behalf of her "Brothers." Only with the passing of time was her soul gradually illumined, and then she perceived intuitively that other souls might follow her and would indeed follow her.

The first divine hint at this fruit of her vocation of love came on August 17th, 1934, when Jesus told her:

When you will have uttered your last 'Jesus, Mary, I love You! Save souls!' I will gather it up and will convey it by means of your life's writings to millions of souls who, though they be sinners, will welcome it and will follow you in the simple way of trust and love, and in that way will love Me.

On November 27th, 1935, He added:

Have no fear. On your dying day you will have attained the summit and will have pronounced the last act of love which Jesus desired when He called you to become a victim of love.

On December 14th, 1935, Our Lord explained to Sister Consolata the reason for changing her spiritual director and intimated that her apostolate was to find its fulfillment in some special work:

Do you know why I have desired this change in your spiritual direction? It is because Father X will make all My desires his own and will bring the work to completion in the manner in which I wish it.

When Sister Consolata repeated these words to her new spiritual director, she admitted to him that she did "not understand to what work Jesus was alluding."

God's works all follow an identical pattern: a hidden preparation, small and humble beginnings, then a sure growth which can overcome the inevitable trials. It was the same with the work of the Littlest Ones. Not only did it originate in the silence of a convent and in the concealment of a soul, but it remained veiled even to that soul when the seed was already present. No, Sister Consolata did not discern the stupendous fruit which Jesus wished to gather from her vocation of love, that is, from her unceasing act of love. She did not know of the work which was to enroll souls by the million all over the world until Jesus deigned to speak of it. Nor did He even then bring her out of her concealment but rather plunged her into still more complete self-effacement.

Before going into the beginnings of this work, it is necessary, however, to clarify the importance of this term. We call it a work because Jesus called it that and because it is one in fact, but not in the sense that it is some kind of association with registration requirements, certificates, etc. . . No. As we have explained before, it is essentially a spiritual way which is, therefore, open to all souls who feel called to embrace it. There is no need for formalities or distinction of persons.

However, it is none the less an institution on this account, for the souls who follow this road are not floundering in uncertainties, each on her own, but they find themselves truly united by the bond of an identical vocation to love and an identical response to that vocation: the unceasing act of love. Without knowing one another or anything about one another, and perhaps without ever meeting here on earth, the Littlest Ones nevertheless constitute in truth a moral entity; in the Church they form a select army which is compact and very active in the spiritual renewal of the world.

Here is how the work originated. On July 4th, 1936, the first Saturday of the month, Jesus gave Sister Consolata to understand during her meditation:

Among the youngest members of Catholic Action there

are the Little Ones. And among the Little Souls there are the Littlest Ones. You belong to these; and to them will belong all those souls who will follow you in offering Me the unceasing act of love.

Jesus is the Divine Word, "all things were made by Him";[1] He is the substantial Word which creates what It decrees: "He spoke and they were made."[2] With the above words He established the Littlest Way of Love and created in the bosom of the Church the Littlest Souls and gave life to the work which must unite them.

A few days later, on July 22nd, the feast of Saint Mary Magdalen, Jesus returned to the subject of the Littlest Ones in these words:

I am not asking you to write down these things for yourself who are about to descend into your grave, but for your Brothers and for the enormous number of Littlest Souls who will follow you in offering Me the unceasing act of love. O Consolata, do you remember your great passion to bring children to Jesus and Jesus to children?[3] Well, you will be bringing children to Me even when you are in heaven, the Littlest Ones, and you will be giving Me to them through your unceasing act of love. Do you believe that?

She did believe it, but:

"O Jesus, but I am doing nothing!"

That does not matter. It is I who am doing everything!

Before the end of that glorious day, and while Sister Consolata was still under the impression of the great divine gift, Jesus added:

---

1. John 1:3.
2. Psalm 32:9.
3. This was the great passion of Pierina Betrone when she was active in the ranks of Catholic Action.

Did I not tell you that you would be loaded down with My graces until you could bear no more? You see, I am keeping My Word. But you must believe in Me!

On July 27th, 1936, Sister Consolata informed her spiritual director of the matter in the following words:

". . . In my diary you will some day read about many divine favors. I cannot conceal from you that on the feast of Saint Mary Magdalen I received great enlightenment and came to understand that Jesus had not forgotten the great passion of my childhood and girlhood to bring children to Jesus. Jesus made me write things down 'for a huge number of Littlest Souls who will follow me by giving Him the unceasing act of love.' So, even from heaven I will be leading the Littlest Ones to Him. My mission will be for the Brothers, and my vocation will be to bring the Littlest Ones to Jesus. . . See what Jesus can do! While He annihilates Consolata in self-effacement, He brings to bloom all the flowers of past renunciations. And while the grain rots underground, Jesus prepares a brilliant, beautiful, and marvelous apostolate! Oh, I believe in Jesus, and with His grace I desire to believe in Him to my last breath, even though I die in the consciousness of having done nothing, absolutely nothing, for the great King, but to love Him, believe in Him, and trust in Him!"

THE CONSECRATION OF THE FIRST LITTLEST ONE

Although the first Saturday of July, 1936, was the day on which Jesus revealed and instituted the Littlest Way of Love and the work which was to give it concrete form, the work itself was not officially begun until two months later, on the First Friday of September, when the first Littlest One, Giovanna Compaire, was consecrated to the Sacred Heart of Jesus.

And so that there might be no doubt as to the meaning of "Littlest One," which refers to the soul and not to the age (in the early days even Sister Consolata was mistaken in this), The Good God disposed that the first Littlest One was to be of the not exactly tender age of 85 years, and not a Religious, though she had preserved her virginity. This was to demonstrate precisely that the Littlest Way of Love is not the privilege of a certain class of persons, but a gift which the Sacred Heart of Jesus bestows on all souls. Here is how the Heart of Jesus communicated the gift of her election to this soul.

Giovanna Compaire had been born and raised in Turin, and for many years directed a well-run shoe store. In 1931, at the age of 80, she gave up the business and retired to a small boarding house conducted by Dominican nuns not far from the Capuchin convent. She was happy there, for she had Jesus in the Blessed Sacrament under the same roof. Her whole life was dedicated to prayer and charity.

At the beginning of October 1934 Father X preached the Forty Hour devotions in the Capuchin church, and Giovanna attended. At the close of the Triduum she addressed to that priest a letter filled with exalted concepts and ended it thus: "Pray for me who hunger so much for God!" In reply the priest paid her a visit; God was uniting these two souls for His merciful ends, and that holy relationship was never broken. It grew rapidly into a spiritual one of father and daughter. Their talks were not frequent, but from each one the priest returned astounded and humiliated. How true it is that God reveals Himself to the little ones! They spoke only of God, for Giovanna's spirit lived in Him and she sought Him in unfailing daily Communion; she sought Him also in frequent visits to the Blessed Sacrament in the little boarding house chapel; and she sought Him through unceasing prayer.

And still she felt that she lacked something which would further intensify her life of love and prayer and cleanse her love from a residue of diffidence.

Then suddenly, seized by grace, Giovanna Compaire found her way, and the Heart of Jesus had made Its first conquest for the ranks of the Littlest Ones.

A few days later, on August 31st, 1936, she wrote to the priest:

"I must tell you, Father, that I have found my place in the throng of Littlest Souls who, like little gnats, buzz about the Cross of Jesus, trying to alight on Him so as to suck vitality from Him. The term "Littlest One" has for me an extraordinary enchantment. Merely to pronounce it brings radiance into my soul, points out a new way for me, and forms my unconquerable defense against the vain and foolish temptations of self-love, etc. . . Could this be a figment of my imagination? I cannot believe that, for I would never have thought it possible to find in this world the tranquillity, security, and freedom which my soul finds there... I am thinking of coming to your church even before next Sunday, for I have need to confer with you. . ."

Before Sunday . . . Jesus, the Divine Heart, who wished to institute the new work on the First Friday of the month, was acting within her. The interview was a short one:

"Tell me, Father, what I must do in order to enter the ranks of the Littlest Ones . . . to enter officially. I do not know, but it seems to me that Jesus desires something from me... I do not know how to express myself..."

The priest was greatly astonished, for he had never given the possibility any thought that the work might be started even before Sister Consolata's death. He replied:

"Well, suppose we do this: tomorrow, being the First Friday of the month, I will come to your boarding house and will celebrate Mass there after the community Mass. You will make your Communion, and directly afterwards you will consecrate yourself as a Littlest One to the Sacred Heart of Jesus through Mary Most Holy, and you will promise from then on to employ all your spiritual energy in the unceasing act of love and in the two other points of the Littlest Way of Love. From the altar, and upon the altar, I will offer your consecration to the Sacred Heart of Jesus."

And so it was done. After the Mass they recited the *Magnificat* together in thanksgiving. The work of the Littlest Ones which Jesus had promised to Sister Consolata had been officially inaugurated.

SISTER CONSOLATA AND THE WORK OF THE LITTLEST ONES

And Sister Consolata? On that Thursday evening, after the above mentioned talk between the priest and Giovanna Compare, the former hastened to acquaint her with the matter in a brief note and recommend it to her prayers. Sister Consolata entered in her diary:

"Gifts are offered on the vigil of a feast. Jesus knows that, and so He gave me the first Littlest One on the vigil of the First Friday of September. What divine and delicate sentiment! Father has harvested this first Littlest One, and tomorrow he will offer her to the Most Sacred Heart of Jesus at Holy Communion. O Jesus, how good Thou art! Truly, Thou dost think of everything, and to me Thou leavest but one thought: to love Thee! Thanks be to Thee, O Jesus!"

It is easy to imagine in what prayerful fervor she passed the day. Jesus, for His part, did not fail to give her further illumination concerning her work, all the more so since she had imagined, at the first mention of Littlest Ones, that it was a question of real children. She could not help smiling when she heard from the priest that the first Littlest One was over eighty years old. Jesus told her:

The Littlest Ones will not merely be counted by the thousands, but by millions and millions. They will not belong exclusively to the feminine sex; there will also be men; yes, there are many Little Souls even among men!

And after your death the Littlest Souls will come running to you just as the children of your catechism class, the Benjamins, came running to you one day in the great St. Maxim Square.[4]

On the evening of that First Friday Sister Consolata entered in her diary:

"This entire day has been dedicated to the Littlest Ones. This evening, at the feet of Jesus solemnly exposed in the Blessed Sacrament, I embraced in spirit all the Littlest Ones throughout the centuries, and I consecrated them all in anticipation to the Sacred Heart of Jesus and asked Him to shelter them all in the depths of His Heart, to watch over them there that not one might be lost, and then to consume

---

4. Pierina Betrone belonged to the parish of Saint Maxim which formed a part of the Association of Feminine Catholic Youth, "Consolatrix."

them in the divine flame, and to grant to each of them to die for love of Him!"

Jesus accepted her prayer and granted it:

Yes, Consolata, the hearts of the Littlest Ones are destined to die of love for Me and to consume themselves exclusively for Me. The world cannot call Me cruel, for ever so many die of vice, victims of the world! Is it not right, Consolata, that the creature should consume herself for her Creator?

THE LITTLEST ONES AND OUR LADY

We now come to point out another instance of how admirably the Heart of Jesus prepares and directs events even to the smallest circumstances, for it is important. Note that the work of the Littlest Ones was officially instituted on the First Friday of September, during the Novena of Our Lady's Nativity. The significance of this providential coincidence is obvious. A work which Jesus Himself termed marvelous and of so great and universal importance for the salvation and sanctification of souls, could not be begun without some sign and pledge of protection on the part of her whose name, together with that of Jesus, is unceasingly invoked by the Littlest Souls. The love for Jesus and the love for Mary are united in the same perennial praise and in the same prayer on behalf of souls.

So it was a part of God's design that this new work should be born at a time when the Church was preparing to celebrate the day on which the most exalted of all creatures appeared littlest upon earth. And not only littlest in her humanity, but even more so in her spirit. The Blessed Virgin alone could in reality make herself littlest, she who was so great in the eyes of God. But we who have contracted the disease of sin, no matter how deeply we may humble ourselves, we will never reach that meanest degree, that littleness, that nothingness, in which we find ourselves before God. Only Mary Most Holy was a true and perfect Littlest One in the particular sense of which we here treat, for she alone made of her life, from its first to its last instant, an unceasing act of love toward God, an act of charity toward her neighbor, and a constant "yes" to the will of God.

That is why the Heart of Jesus wished the work to be initiated on the First Friday of September. It was to be like a flower that opened in bloom at the feet of this heavenly babe to receive the dew of her first smile, the warmth of her first blessing, as a pledge of success and of perennial duration.

Sister Consolata, in her tender love for the Virgin, could not fail to notice these circumstances and felt herself intimately and irresistibly driven to consecrate the Littlest Ones not only to the Heart of Jesus, but also to that of Our Blessed Lady. She writes:

"Because the first of these souls has consecrated herself among the Littlest Ones to-day, on the First Friday of September, during the Novena to the Nativity of Mary Most Holy, I shall embrace all the Littlest Ones of all the ages on Tuesday next, September 8th, and I will place them next to her cradle and consecrate them to the infant Mary. She will protect them, will favor them, will keep them under her mantle always, just as she does with Sister Consolata. And the Littlest Ones will love Our Lady deeply because the unceasing act of love which they offer to Jesus is also intended for Mary Most Holy."

THE LITTLEST ONES AND SISTER CONSOLATA

With the consecration of the Littlest Ones to the Heart of Jesus and Mary Most Holy, Sister Consolata's particular task came to an end as far as that work and her interest in its diffusion were concerned, for she was not to lessen the continuity and virginity of her love, nor the self-effacement which Jesus desired. For that reason He told her on July 31st, 1936, after revealing the work to her:

Love Me; give Me this unceasing act of love; and I promise you that you will give Me all your Brothers one by one, and then also the Littlest Ones.

Then, when the work had made an actual beginning, Our Lord intervened again so that Sister Consolata would not have to neglect her act of love:

Forget yourself, Consolata. Do not think about yourself or about what you might term your special vocation. No. The Heart of Jesus has made use of you as of a tool (as you would use a broom), but this marvelous work of the Littlest Ones will be brought to completion solely by the Heart of Jesus. Therefore, you must think only of giving Me the unceasing act of love, your 'yes' to everything and everybody, and of accepting suffering with gratitude. Nothing else! I will think of everything; you must forget yourself!

On September 8th, 1936, He said:

Now that you have consecrated the Littlest Ones to the infant Mary, you must think no more about the Littlest Ones except in your daily prayer. Think solely of the Brothers and Sisters whom you shall lead back to Me through the unceasing act of love.

But even if it was not permitted to Sister Consolata to occupy herself directly with this work, she nevertheless belongs to it, and it is upon her that the Littlest Ones fix their eyes, as Jesus predicted in September 1937:

Do not interrupt your act of love. Proceed along your road, unconcerned about the enemy's designs! Have no fear! Keep advancing always! Love conquers everything.

I desire a wave of love to ascend from earth to heaven. You must tread the Littlest Way as the first one. One day you will have to serve as a model. Just as the world now looks upon the Little Flower, so will millions of Littlest Ones all over the world look upon you!

We shall close with two comforting promises, the one made by Jesus, and the other by Our Lady. On July 14th, 1936, at a time when Sister Consolata felt herself deeply humiliated and embarrassed by so many divine favors, she turned to Jesus:

"But Thou art loving them passionately, these Littlest Ones!"

Yes, Our Lord replied, *they are the pupils of My eye!*

On September 8th, 1942, Sister Consolata reconsecrated the Littlest Ones to the Immaculate Virgin, and the latter gave her to understand that she was pleased with the gift:

"Upon all, and upon each one, I will look with predilection, as I have done with you!"

THE DEATH OF THE FIRST LITTLEST ONE

If any doubt could still exist as to the divine origin and the excellence of the Littlest Way of Love, the remaining months of Giovanna Compaire's life and her death would suffice to dissipate it. Her spiritual growth was admirable and her flight to sanctity rapid and sure. She no longer dreaded the heights now that her soul had become one of the Littlest Ones and had grown the wings of love and confidence. Uncertainty, fear, vain concern about herself, all disappeared as if by magic. The divine Artist knew that time was short, and so He brought His masterpiece to completion with a few strokes. On October 13th, 1936, one short month after her consecration as a Littlest One, Giovanna wrote to her spiritual director:

". . . I would like to tell you something about how I pass my days and also certain night hours since I received the great graces. I seem to be living in another world! The thought of the fourth of September with its *Magnificat* brings more tears to my eyes now, but they are no more the tears of before. My trust in God now rests solely upon the merits of Our Lord Jesus Christ. . . And He lets me experience the community of saints through the efficacy of their prayers! . . . Everything transports and envelops me in a profusion of marvels which gives a profound peace to my life."

In the new way, Giovanna found the holy liberty of a true child of God. Love relieved her of the weary burden of herself. Now she sustained everything, or better said, she thought no more about herself. Everything in her spiritual life was now simplified and had a new perfection. She found that the unceasing act of love contained everything, gave everything, obtained everything. She experienced that the summit was luminous and restful and at the same time a divine means for ascending to further heights. On the feast of Mary's Nativity in 1937, that is one year after her consecration as a Littlest One, Giovanna renewed that same consecration with the following prayer which was also to be her "nunc dimittis":

"O Mary Immaculate, my powerful advocate and most tender Mother, behold me prostrate at your feet in order to renew the act by which I am consecrated to the Most Sacred Heart of Jesus as a Littlest One. My every thought and affection, my heart and all my life, are for Jesus and for you! On this blessed day on which the Church recalls your appearance among us... I pray you, deign to take under your special protection the new work of the Littlest Ones of Jesus. That work crystallizes the marvelous and miraculous *laus perennis* (perennial praise) of children, which your divine Son has shown Himself to delight in and to bless with the most sublime graces of His divine Heart. To your immaculate heart I confide my consolations and my pains, my fears and my hopes, by offering the unceasing act of love. Obtain for me that I may conclude my life as Jesus has given His, in homage to the Most Holy Trinity and to you for ever and ever."

Giovanna felt that heaven was indeed near. Her strength was waning, but she did not fail to come downstairs each morning for Mass and Holy Communion, and to pay several visits during the day to Jesus in the Blessed Sacrament. There was still a youthful freshness in her parchment-like features which were almost free from wrinkles even at 87 years. She was consumed more by love than by years. When Jesus in the Holy Eucharist was exposed, the divine Host appeared radiant to her eyes, though they were sightless to everything else. In the depth of her heart, too, mysterious voices made themselves heard like the whispers of the approaching Spouse...

She was ready; with the minutest care she had arranged

everything so as to give Sister Death a good reception. The Capuchin Sisters had the habit of their order ready in which she wished to be clothed after death.

On January 26th, 1938, while alone in her room and absorbed in prayer, she felt herself overcome by an extraordinary effusion of grace; her whole being trembled, and an uncontainable urge seized her to declare her love to God, to give Him thanks, to reach Him, to become transformed into Him! . . . Falling upon her knees, her arms raised, her face bathed in tears, she exclaimed: "My God, my God, what is this?"

It was her call to heaven. On Sexagesima Sunday, February 20th, 1938, she came downstairs to Mass for the last time. On the Wednesday following she received Extreme Unction with clear consciousness. Then followed three days and three nights in which she was with Jesus on the Cross, suffering mysterious spasms without respite. But not one lament was heard. To her spiritual director she confided:

"When I meditated on the Passion of Our Lord Jesus Christ, I always lingered especially on His agonizing spasms. I believe that now He is permitting me to share in them."

Then, turning her eyes towards the Cruxifix on the opposite wall, she repeated with an incredible transport of love what had been her watchword in life:

"To love Thee, to follow Thee, to imitate Thee!"

Someone remarked that soon she would be receiving her reward for so many good deeds:

"Deeds, no. I have done nothing! But that I have loved Jesus much, above everything else, that yes! That is what consoles me!"

Sisters of various religious congregations and priests came to her bedside to visit with her and pray for her.

"Jesus is faithful. I have always refused the friendships of the world, and He has surrounded me with holy friendships."

When Holy Viaticum was solemnly brought to her on Friday evening, she begged forgiveness for any scandal she had given. The sighs and tears of those about her were her reply. She was speaking of having given scandal—she whose virtue could be admired by all!

On Saturday afternoon her suffering seemed to reach its height.

"Are you suffering much, Giovanna?"

"Yes. I would never have thought it possible that a mere creature could suffer like this. But do not grieve over it, Father, for I have great need to suffer!"

Later on, she seemed suddenly relieved, her body reacted no longer to pain. But she was not deceived:

"It is the betterment which precedes the climax."

She actually spoke and acted as though she were cured. That evening the Holy Rosary was, therefore, prayed in her room, and at the fourth glorious mystery, the Assumption of Mary, she commented:

"In heaven, body and soul! How beautiful and consoling is this profession of faith on the point of death!"

She led the fifth mystery herself:

"Let us contemplate Mary, the Comforter of the Afflicted."

During the night her pain returned, and at about two o'clock she received Holy Communion for the last time. Her mind remained marvelously lucid almost to the end. This came at the stroke of one on the afternoon of Quinquagesima Sunday, February 27th, 1938. She had made a prayerful Sign of the Cross, and after a short agony this first Littlest

One sweetly reclined her head upon the Heart of Jesus, there to remain forever and to continue her canticle of love: "Jesus, Mary, I love You! Save souls!"

SISTER CONSOLATA'S MESSAGE TO THE LITTLEST ONES

Concerning the death of the first Littlest One, Sister Consolata wrote:

"I do not know why, but ever since this dear soul has winged her way to heaven, I am completely pervaded by a wave of joy, an intense joy, and by light, oh what light! Jesus has given my soul greater strength and grace, greater perseverance in the unceasing act of love, and a real longing for solitude and silence. As a result, I am confident that all this will aid me to suffer well and to give to Jesus the fruit He desires."

The work of the Littlest Ones did not decline with the death of the first member, nor did the continuous act of love become extinguished outside the Capuchin convent. The Heart of Jesus had meanwhile issued Its call to other souls, and the Littlest Ones already formed a group of some twenty Sisters and women members of Catholic Action, and even a small representation of men.

On their behalf and for those of the coming centuries, Sister Consolata's spiritual director requested a letter from her in which she would expound her own thoughts on how to practice the unceasing act of love and offer some practical advice. We reproduce this letter almost in its entirety, and every Littlest One may consider it to have been written expressly for her or for him. Its content is all the more valuable since it has found confirmation in Sister Consolata's own life which will hardly ever be surpassed in continuity and virginity of love.

Dearest Littlest One of the Heart of Jesus

"When you go to rest in the evening, you should ask your good guardian angel to love Jesus on your behalf while you are asleep, to awaken you in the morning, and to inspire you to the act of love. If you will be faithful in asking this of him each evening, he will be faithful in awakening you every morning with a 'Jesus, Mary, I love You! Save souls!'

"Begin your day in this way, and continue to love until you meet Jesus in the Holy Eucharist. That does not mean that you should neglect all other prayers. No! Carry on your usual practices of piety, but do not add any others. Let your act of love absorb your every spare moment, and in the future even some of your vocal prayers if Jesus so inspires you.

"In Holy Communion entrust and abandon yourself to Jesus, your troubles, projects, desires, and sorrows, and then think no more about them. For the whole life of a Littlest One is based upon this divine promise: *I will think of everything, even to the least detail; you must think only of loving Me!* Copy these words out under an image of the Sacred Heart, and do it in such a way that they will be always in sight. They will be a great help to you in freeing your spirit from all preoccupation, and you will experience in yourself how faithfully Jesus keeps His promise.

"After having abandoned everything to Jesus during Holy Communion, renew to Him your promise of the unceasing act of love, your 'yes' to everything He will demand of you throughout the day, and determine to see Him, to speak with Him, and to serve Him lovingly in all His creatures with whom you will come in contact.

"Form your intention once and for all that your every act of love may ascend to heaven as a supplication, to implore fidelity for yourself in persevering uninterruptedly until your next Communion, and that it be in reparation for your every infidelity.

"As you leave the church, begin with your act of love, and continue it on your way, at home, and while carrying out each of your duties. Remember that Jesus has given His promise that while you are writing, or praying, or meditating, or while you must speak out of necessity or charity, your act of love will continue just the same.

"Arrange to have before you, if possible, while you work an image or a card with the words: 'Jesus, Mary, I love You! Save souls!' This will serve as a reminder to you.

"Among the obstacles which prevent you from offering Jesus the unceasing virginal act of love, Our Lord teaches us to combat three: useless thoughts, useless talk, and outside interests. As for thoughts and preoccupations, everything becomes useless from the moment that Jesus promises His Littlest One that He Himself will think of everything, even to the smallest details. As for useless talk, if you speak when you are not obliged to do so out of necessity, charity or propriety, then it is a waste of time; you steal time from Love. As for extraneous interests, curiosity, etc., all these detach your spirit from the one thing to which you have vowed yourself: to love Jesus unceasingly and with a virginal love.

"It is necessary, however, for you to realize that, to carry out the divine wishes, never to lose one act of love or one act of charity from one Communion to another, will require arduous work from your soul (sustained by grace), no small amount of time, and a generous, constant effort; above all, never let yourself become discouraged.

"At every more or less voluntary infidelity, renew your determination of virginal love, and start afresh. If your fault causes you suffering, you should offer it to Jesus . . . as an act of love! You will see and will be able to experience with what tenderness Jesus raises you up again after each fall or infidelity, how He hastens to put you on your feet again, so that you may continue your canticle of love.

"What will aid you most in offering Jesus the unceasing act of love, is to renew your resolution at every hour and to make a particular examen of your conscience concerning it. Keep in mind that in this particular examen about the unceasing act of love you are to note as faults only the time which you have wasted in useless talk or in following your imagination, vain thoughts, etc. . . Make good your shortcomings, and then take up your loving again with tranquillity.

"The resolution, however, to which you must consecrate all your energies should always concern the unceasing act of love. Have no fear! Jesus will aid you. He has said: *I ask only one thing of you: an unceasing act of love. . . Love Me, for I thirst for your love. . . Love Me, and you will be happy; the more you will love Me, the happier you will be!* . . . Jesus keeps His word!

"So, have courage! Jesus and Mary will aid you! Never have any fear, but trust and believe in the love which He has for you!"

Affectionately,

Sister Consolata, R.C.

TO ALL WHO ARE NOT LITTLEST ONES

That is what Sister Consolata wrote to the Littlest Ones. But now we address ourselves to all those, and they are in the majority, who at this point will declare: "All well and good; this is sublime; but I am terrified by that unceasing act of love!"

We have already explained how the continuity of love should be understood, and that it is the effort which counts with God. But it must be admitted that relatively few souls are called to follow Sister Consolata in her perfection of the Littlest Way of Love, that is, in the unceasing and virginal act of love. It is true that Jesus foretold that they would be counted by the millions, but that is to be understood in the succession of time across the centuries. In the bosom of Mother Church the Littlest Ones will, therefore, always form a "pusillus grex," a small flock.

Nevertheless, the new message of the Heart of Jesus is under certain aspects addressed to all souls, and to all it can become a source of great good. In fact its doctrine, that the act of love is a valuable means to sanctification and the apostolate, is of interest to all souls without exception. Therefore, those who cannot offer the act of love unceasingly, can still avail themselves of it for making progress in the interior life, for this is essentially a life of love. In other words, to a few souls, the Littlest Ones, Sister Consolata says: "Follow me with your efforts to transform your life into one act of unceasing love." To all others she says: "Avail yourselves of my act of love in the measure in which it is possible for you."

Whether one desires it or not, one needs some means for avoiding or combating the dissipation caused mostly by thoughts, extraneous interests, useless words. Each soul is free to choose what is suitable for her and appeals most to her spirit. It should be noted, however, that as love is the first and most excellent of all virtues, so the act of love (no matter how formulated, just so long as it comes from the heart), shares this great excellence. So why not give the preference to that means which is the most excellent, the one dearest to Jesus, the one which is most profitable to the soul? We need not stress the fact that Sister Consolata's act of love and its formula is invested with a particular value because it comes from Jesus and because it joins to the love of Jesus a love for Our Blessed Lady and a love for souls.

Such an act is, therefore, available to all souls, even those who are not Littlest Ones. They can use the act as a simple ejaculation to be recited frequently during the day, either vocally or silently, but always from the heart. An effort should be made to give value through the act to the many free minutes throughout the day which would otherwise be lost in useless or even dangerous thoughts. Even if a soul does not succeed in giving to the Good God more than say ten acts during the day (which would certainly not require any great effort), how large would be their number after a month, or a year! Meanwhile, as it becomes a habit, it will not be difficult to gradually increase the number until, day by day, one gains a certain facility in offering the act, and therefore, a more continuous union with Jesus.

Such was the intention of the Sacred Heart of Jesus when It dictated the doctrine of the act of love to Sister Consolata; for Jesus suggested the act of love not only to the Littlest Souls, but also to the young in age and to all those persons who cannot offer an unceasing act, but only a frequent one. An act may not be unceasing with respect to one soul, but it becomes so when it is offered up by many souls simultaneously. In this way, little by little, there will rise collectively in every part of the world an unceasing wave of love, and this in turn will become transformed into a descending wave of unceasing love, of mercy, and of pardon.

THE UNCEASING ACT OF LOVE AND THE PRACTICE OF VIRTUE

Many may wonder to what point the unceasing act of love carried Sister Consolata in the practice and perfection of Christian and religious virtues. That is a legitimate question, for one cannot form a definite judgment about a certain doctrine without first seeing the fruits in those who follow it. Although it is the purpose of this book to expound the doctrine of the unceasing act of love, rather than to treat of Sister Consolata's virtues, we have already shown that she possessed unusual virtue in trying to eliminate from her path everything that could prove to be a hindrance in following Jesus as perfectly as possible.

In any case we must bear in mind that the act of unceasing love, though of prime importance to the Littlest Way of Love, does not in itself fulfill it completely; it must also embrace the two other points which Jesus indicated to Sister Consolata: a smiling "yes" for everyone, seeing Jesus in all, and a thankful "yes" to everything that Our Lord demands of the soul.

In that lies the practical fruit of the life of love, that we exercise perfect charity toward our neighbor and accept

God's dispositions concerning ourselves in a spirit of complete sacrifice and with a full response to grace. It is easy to see that a soul who maintains herself heroically faithful to these three points will advance securely and rapidly in every other virtue. That is what Jesus promised to Sister Consolata:

Remain always in your act of love; try not to omit one, and try also not to miss one act of charity. Gather with love the flowers of virtue which I will cause to bloom along your path, and the fruit which you will bring Me will be abundant. (September 26th, 1935)

With the unceasing act of love you will attain the longed-for summit of love; with your 'yes' to everything, the summit of sorrow; and these two peaks will generate the third, that of the souls. (June 21st, 1942)

These brief indications should suffice to persuade us that the path followed by Sister Consolata, if understood and practiced in its entirety, is not based solely on sentiment, but embraces a true and complete program for the spiritual life of the highest Christian and religious perfection.

- VIII -

SUMMARY

BACK TO THE SOURCE

IT does not behoove us to make any pronouncement on this *Message*. We are only its transmitters. It is the Church which must authenticate its truthfulness. But every reader may form his own opinion as to its value in achieving the end for which it was dictated: to bring the world back to the source of every moral resurgence and all social well-being, the Gospel of Our Lord Jesus Christ.

The true and complete Gospel teaches us not only to believe, but also to hope, and above all, to love.

In this sense, besides being a written book, the Gospel is the living word of those who saw and heard the Master, who listened to His message, as Saint John says,[1] a message of reconciliation with God through the expiatory sacrifice of Jesus,[2] and therefore, of grace and of friendship with Him.

The prophet Jeremias foretold the work of the messianic age with this call to the inner life: "Behold the days shall

---

1. I John 1:5; and 3:11.
2. I John 2:2.

come, saith the Lord, and I will make a new covenant with the house of Israel, and with the house of Juda: not according to the covenant which I made with their fathers, in the day I took them by the hand to bring them out of the land of Egypt: the covenant which they made void, and I had dominion over them, saith the Lord. But this shall be the covenant that I will make with the house of Israel, after those days, saith the Lord: I will give My Law in their bowels, and I will write it in their heart: and I will be their God, and they shall be My people."[3]

Saint Paul proves this prophecy to have been fulfilled.[4] The Gospel, therefore, does not wish to be merely a law written on papyrus, or one of external observance, but a law which touches and interests us deeply. It was written in our hearts by the Holy Spirit, the "Finger of God," with the effusion of a new life, the life of grace and of love, and without this the very letter of the Gospel would kill, as Saint Augustine well observes.

This transmission of new life affects our intelligence which accepts the doctrine of the Catholic Church on faith; it fulfills itself in the very depths of the human spirit through the use of the sacraments which give us grace; it has its divine pulsation in the heart through the charity which establishes a life of friendship with Him,[5] and so there is fulfilled in us the great saying of the prophet which is repeated by Saint Paul:

"And I will be their God, and they shall be My people."[6]

---

3. Jeremias 31:31-33.
4. Hebrews 8:8-10.
5. John 15:12-15.
6. Jeremias 31:33.

THE LAW OF LOVE

Since it is a fact that God is Love,[7] His law can be no other than a law of love. If we substitute a faith in that which pleases us for a faith in divine authority, and a religious experience for love, then we destroy the principle on which the hope of life is founded, and we annul the primacy of the great commandment which Jesus reconfirmed; Christian life is emptied of its content.

Then the second commandment will also become adulterated, being similar to the first,[8]—God in our neighbor. As a result, all other commandments also lose their consistency, since they are merely ramifications of the first two; and then we have chaos! Then *believing* will also become extinct, because contempt for the law always rebounds upon the legislator; and behold, we have intellectual chaos!

The moral and intellectual decay in the world to-day derives its origin, therefore, firstly from the fact that the Gospel was adulterated by changing the order which God desired: the supremacy of spiritual values and Christian duties. As an unescapable consequence, the Gospel was emptied of all divine authority and all ethical content until it became reduced to a philosophical system of purely historical value. That is why the pseudo-reformation of the sixteenth century not only shattered the unity of the Christian people, but sowed the seeds of all the subsequent errors and apostasies. One cannot mutilate the Gospel without also

---

7. I John 4:16.
8. Matthew 22:39.

mutilating the Church, and vice versa. A mutilated Gospel is no longer a Gospel. "Whosoever shall keep the whole law, but offend in one point, is become guilty of all."[9] All the more so when it concerns the point of departure, the very foundation and purpose of the whole Law.

The Gospel cannot be repudiated with impunity, as the world has found out through sad experience.

THE EVIL AND ITS REMEDY

So much for the field of cockle. Now what about the good grain? It would be a great mistake to maintain that what we have said about the life of love could in some way lessen the need and importance of action in all its outward manifestations. This writer is no hermit but a missionary, and for that matter, hermits do not stand idle with folded hands either.

We would merely like to ask how it comes that we have not succeeded in damming the rising and inundating flood of evil which threatens to submerge the world? Were we too little active? To us it does not seem so. We may regret individual deficiencies, but on the whole, there was organic, vigorous and many-sided action. Was it not adapted to the needs of our times? That too cannot be maintained, at least as far as the whole of Catholic activity is concerned. What then? The defect is this, it seems to us, that on the one hand the *living flame* of the sower has been lacking: "Without Me

---

9. James 2:10.

you can do nothing."[10] On the other hand there has been an absence of good topsoil to receive and fertilize the good seed: "He that abideth in Me, and I in Him, the same beareth much fruit."[11]

To dwell in Jesus, that is what is needful to the soul above everything else, both for doing good and for receiving good and making her bear fruit. Now, *to dwell* in Jesus implies more than believing in Him, or being in the state of grace: it means to live the life of grace, to make it grow, and to perfect it continually within us.[12] And that is achieved through our union with Jesus by drawing from Him as the branch from the vine, the divine life-blood which makes all Christian virtues fruitful. Love, the life of love, brings all this about: "As the Father hath loved Me, I also have loved you. Abide in My love."[13] Love vivifies the faith of the believer who comes to the Father through Jesus.

When Pius XI addressed his encyclical on Spiritual Exercises to the world at the beginning of this period of world history, and when Pius XII sent out his encyclicals on the Mystical Body and on the Sacred Liturgy, superficial minds failed to see the connection between these papal documents and the needs of the Christian world. But these pronouncements were and are in perfect focus on the exigencies of our times, for they uncover the real cause of all the evils and point to a more intense supernatural life of souls as their remedy.

Saint Paul said of himself, as though explaining the ardor of his untiring zeal: "The charity of Christ presseth

---

10. John 15:5.
11. John 15:5.
12. John 10:10.
13. John 15:9.

us."[14] These are the very words which Saint Joseph Cottolengo placed over the entrance door to that "Little House of Divine Providence" which is probably the greatest charitable institution the world has ever known; it is a splendid defense of Christianity, of Christianity which is lived, of Christianity which is love: *Charitas Christi*. The Little Flower has left us only the few pages of her *Story of a Soul*, but these were written by one who was throbbing with love and with suffering for Jesus and for souls. How much good these pages have already done! And how much more will they still do until the end of the world! It is the same with all other forms of the apostolate. When a soul draws strength and enthusiasm from Jesus "full of grace and truth"[15] and makes of her life an example of light like "a burning and shining light,"[16] then the works bear testimony to the Truth and communicate to other souls the ardor with which they are animated. We cannot give what we do not possess. On the contrary: "What I have, I give thee; in the Name of Jesus Christ of Nazareth, arise and walk."[17] This is what the world stands in need of, if it is to rise again and take up once more its ascent: it has need of souls who are filled with Jesus in order to give Jesus.

The informative spirit of this *Message* lies entirely in this, that it makes us understand the need for a profound interior life, which is essentially a life of love, and the need to sanctify ourselves and others.

---

14. II Corinthians 5:14.
15. John 1:14.
16. John 5:35.
17. Acts 3:6.

THE NEW GIFT OF THE HEART OF JESUS

Jesus points out the practical means for achieving this end through the Littlest Way of Love and its related work of the Littlest Ones. No one ought to be concerned about the multiplicity of spiritual ways existing in Christian asceticism. This is not really a new way, nor could it be. The Way is a single one for everyone in every age: Jesus. "I am the Way."[18] Sister Consolata follows the Little Flower in the same manner that the latter follows the Gospel; no more, no less. But this way which is always substantially the same, that is, love, can pass through the most varied fields of Christian mysticism and so assume new aspects, new forms, and hence new names. In the same way new institutions are continually arising in the bosom of the Church without damaging in the least her unity of doctrine and structure. In connection with the terms "Littlest Way" and "Littlest Souls" it must be pointed out that these were given by Jesus Himself. In order to make Sister Consolata understand His teaching,[19] He enlightened her about her habitual notions and explained the higher sense in which to use the Church's words. If the Church considers it holy and fruitful to enroll boys and girls who are still very young in years in her hierarchical organism for purposes of the apostolate, then it is only just and proper that the Littlest Souls should also find a place in the organization of her spiritual life.

This is the tangible fruit of this *Message*, that the unceasing act of love be conveyed to souls and propagated throughout the world. We have already told how the doc-

---

18. John 14:6.
19. Matthew 11:25; and 18:3.

trine of the unceasing act of love constitutes the very essence of the new manifestation of the Heart of Jesus. This is, therefore, a gift which Jesus gives to the world and its significance at the present moment should escape no one. Jesus Himself added this, after having foretold to Sister Consolata what immense good would result to the world from the practice of the unceasing act of love:

It was for this purpose that I had you ask each morning that through the merits of My dolorous Passion there might triumph in the world not only My mercy, but particularly My love, and especially so in the Littlest Souls.

God's mercy can pardon, but only His love can renew the world. "Thou shalt send forth Thy Spirit, and they shall be created, and Thou shalt renew the face of the earth."[20] The Church applies these words to the action of the Holy Spirit in the world, who is the spirit of love, or rather Love Itself. A new Pentecost of love will renew the face of the earth spiritually, and the work of the Littlest Ones was decreed by Jesus for just this purpose.

Whoever has followed in these pages Our Lord's continual request for love, His reiterated declaration that He wished to save the world by love, and the divine promises regarding the perennial, universal, and prodigious fruitfulness of this act of unceasing love, cannot doubt but that the work of the Littlest Ones was truly preordained by Divine Providence and Infinite Love to make a powerful contribution to the spiritual rebirth of the world.

Once again God wishes to confound, through the insignificance of the means, the intellectual pride which has obscured so many minds; the poor in spirit bring down the

---

20. Psalm 103:30.

strong men of this earth who think they can erect their own paganizing civilization over the tomb of Christianity. Through a silent but very active life of love God wishes to cure the world of that pernicious modern evil which consists in a great noise of activity without being vivified by the Spirit of God.

Understood in this sense, the new *Message* might be termed a rainbow of peace, projected from the Heart of Jesus upon this poor world which has rejected the springs of the living and health-giving water of the Gospel in favor of the polluted cisterns of evil and error, only to find death and ruin in them. But Jesus desires to save the world, and after having halted it in good time on the perilous brink and having purified it through suffering, He now wishes to bring it back to Himself through love, so that it may experience what Sister Consolata felt all through her life, the truth of the divine words:

Love Me and you will be happy; the more you will love Me, the happier you will be!

God always wins out in this manner, through infinite mercy and infinite love!

TO THEE, O LORD!

Before laying down his pen, O Lord Jesus, Thy servant humbles himself in Thy sight for having dared to add his inadequate human words to what he considers Thy words, and for having perchance spoiled Thy work through his own inability and fault. But Thou art omnipotent, O Lord, and as from nothingness Thou dost bring forth everything, so Thou canst make these very human failings serve to carry out Thy designs. Therefore, to Thee be all praise, honor, and glory!

And as also every effort is in vain which is not blessed by Thee, so I ardently implore that benediction. I ask it for the infinite love which Thou hast for men, Thy creatures, Thy redeemed brothers. I ask it through the intercession of her into whose Immaculate Heart Thou didst pour for us all the health-giving stream which bursts forth from Thy pierced Heart. And I ask it through the prayers of that soul whom Thou didst choose as a messenger of Thy love; who in response to Thy gift of election, and sustained by Thy grace, knew how to consummate her life in an unceasing act of virginal love, in an uninterrupted invocation for the salvation of souls.

Thou didst tell her one day: *When your last "Jesus, Mary, I love You! Save souls!" will have been uttered, I will gather it up and will convey it to millions of souls who, though they be sinners, will receive it and will follow you in the simple way of trust and love, and so will love Me. . . I desire that a wave of love should ascend from the earth to heaven!*

Now that her last act of love has ceased on earth in order to perpetuate itself in heaven, gather Thou it up and convey it to souls, to all souls—to the innocent and to sinners, to those who stray from the Church, and to all who are sighing outside the fold. Make it fruitful through Thy benediction so that it may perpetuate itself on earth, and so that the wave of love which Thou didst invoke may be formed and may grow. Then will men be re-made Thy sons through love, then will they become once again brothers to one another through charity, and the world will finally find again, in Thy Gospel of love and charity, its salvation and the way to its lost tranquillity!

Jesus, Mary, I love You! Save souls!

Appendix

SOME CLARIFICATIONS REGARDING THE WORK OF THE LITTLEST ONES

IN reply to the inquiries which we have received, we give here in catechetical form a few short explanations concerning the Littlest Ones and their work.

Who are the Littlest Ones?

The term "Littlest One" must not be understood as referring to age; it refers to souls. The Littlest Ones are those souls who feel an attraction to follow Sister Consolata in her Littlest Way of Love, that is, in the way of the unceasing act of love.

How is the continuity of the act of love to be understood?

It is understood in relation to the state of life, the occupation, and the capacity of each individual person. It should also be kept in mind that during the time that a person is conversing with someone for reasons of necessity, charity or decency, and while employed in work which absorbs the attention of the mind, then the act of love goes on in the sight of God, provided the soul takes care to direct all her actions to God with an intention. At other times, however, that is during the free minutes throughout the day, the Littlest One should exert every effort to continue the act of love.

Is it necessary to pronounce the act of love with the lips?

No. It suffices to offer it with the heart. The purpose of the unceasing act of love is, in the intention of Jesus, to offer to souls a practical and easy means for achieving the deepest fervor of love for Him. It must not be a formula, therefore, which is repeated mechanically; nor is it the number of acts which count; but it is an unceasing abandonment of the soul to love, an uninterrupted effusion of love, a continuous and silent canticle of love.

Is not such a continuity of love through a fixed formula oppressive to the spirit?

Understood as above, the unceasing act of love has nothing oppressive about it for souls who sincerely desire to live a life of love in all perfection. Besides, Jesus has asked for it, and He has attached a particular unction to it just as He grants a particular grace to the Littlest Ones that they may be faithful to it. Experience has already shown that the more faithful a soul is to it, the more does the act of love become a real need for that soul.

Is it possible to achieve an absolute continuity in the act of love?

Without God's favor it is not possible for human creatures to arrive at an absolute continuity in the act of love. However, sustained by grace, the soul can achieve a moral continuity, that is, she can make the act morally unceasing through the effort of her will—which is all that Jesus asks.

Is it necessary to find pleasure in practicing the act of love?

As with all practices of the spiritual life, so in carrying

out the unceasing act of love, it is not necessary that the soul should find in it a sensible pleasure. The fervor of the will suffices, if sustained by faith in the intrinsic excellence of the act of love and in the requests and promises of Jesus. In fact, it ordinarily happens that the soul does not find any sensible pleasure in it, and that is because God disposes matters so that the act of love may be the more meritorious and more fruitful of good for souls.

In what does the perfection of the unceasing act of love consist?

In this, as in all practices of the spiritual life, the soul can attain to a greater or lesser perfection. That consists principally in the following three requirements of the life of love: continuity of love; that is, to love with an actual love as continuously as possible, ("Thou shalt love the Lord thy God with thy whole heart"):—purity of love; that is, to struggle against useless thoughts, words, and interests, ("Thou shalt love . . . with thy whole mind"):—intensity of love; that is, to give to the act of love all possible intensity, ("Thou shalt love . . . with thy whole soul, and with all thy strength").

What of those who are not called to be Littlest Ones?

The act of love, as a means for progressing in the life of love, is offered by Jesus to all souls of good will without distinction—not then as an unceasing act of love, but as a frequent one.

What formalities are required in order to become one of the Littlest Ones?

No formality whatsoever: no registration, no insignia, nothing of the kind. It is not a question of an association, society, etc., but of a spiritual life which is open to all souls who feel themselves drawn to it.

Is not even a special consecration required?

It is only natural that the soul who feels herself called to this way, should also feel the need of beginning it with a special consecration of herself to Love. It was thus with the first of the Littlest Ones and with the others who have already entered these privileged ranks.

How does one make this consecration?

There is no fixed procedure. Following the example of the first Littlest One, we would suggest the following: a) select a certain day, preferably a feast of Our Lord or of Our Lady or a First Friday of the month; b) prepare yourself by a novena or triduum of deep recollection and prayer; c) on the predetermined day hear Holy Mass, and during Holy Communion offer your own consecration as a Littlest One, confiding it to the Heart of Jesus by the hands of Mary Most Holy; then conclude by reciting the *Magnificat*.

In some special formula of consecration necessary?

No. The soul is free to express her own adhesion to the Littlest Way of Love as best suits her and as the heart dictates.

Could you nevertheless suggest a formula?

Here is one: "Most Sacred Heart of Jesus, who hast loved men so much and dost ask nothing but love from them, I ... (your name) ... , being desirous to assuage the ardent longing of Thy divine Heart, consecrate myself to Thee as one of the Littlest Ones through the hands of the Immaculate

Virgin, and I pledge myself to give Thee an unceasing act of love, to have a smiling 'yes' for everybody, and a thankful 'yes' for everything. O Good Jesus, receive this my act of consecration, submerge it in Thy Most Precious Blood, strengthen it by Thy omnipotent grace, so that I may be faithful to it even unto death, and that the unceasing act of love which I have begun on earth may perpetuate itself forever in heaven. O Sacred Heart of Jesus, thirsting for love and for souls, make me one of Thy little victims of love to cooperate with Thee and with our Mother in the salvation of souls! Amen."

Does such a consecration bind the soul under pain of sin?

Absolutely not! Neither mortal sin nor venial sin; nothing of the kind! Therefore, you would not be committing a fault if you withdrew from the way you had embraced, or if you voluntarily neglected to practice the unceasing act of love. You would be merely depriving yourself of merit.

How should a soul proceed who feels herself attracted to this way?

She ought to proceed slowly, with calmness and reflection, so as to make certain whether such an impulse was the result of God's grace or merely a fleeting enthusiasm. The soul would do well to ask God for enlightenment through more assiduous prayer: and meanwhile she could practice the unceasing act of love for a certain length of time without assuming any formal obligation. Only after she finds out that heart and spirit fare well on this road, and that the interior life derives real benefit from it, only then should the soul make her consecration as one of the Littlest Ones.

PRAYER

FOR OBTAINING GRACES THROUGH THE INTERCESSION OF SISTER CONSOLATA

O Jesus, who didst deign to choose Consolata Betrone as an ardent apostle of Thy Divine Heart in order to diffuse in the world Thy doctrine of the unceasing act of love and to establish the Littlest Way of Love in the Church, we beseech Thee to glorify her on earth as we believe Thou hast already glorified her in heaven, so as to demonstrate to the world the divine origin and efficacy of this new spiritual way. For this purpose and through her intercession we ask Thee for the grace which we have so much at heart, in the firm hope of being heard, if it be for the good of our souls. Jesus, Mary, I love You! Save Souls!

(The Triduum or Novena should be accompanied by prayers and Holy Communion).

❖ ❖ ❖

Jesus, Mary, I love You! Save souls!
300 days indulgence for reciting this ejaculatory prayer.

October 1st, 1949. ✠ M. CARD. FOSSATI,
Archbishop of Turin

❖ ❖ ❖

Anyone receiving graces through the intercession of Consolata Betrone is asked to give notice of them to the following address: Capuchin Convent, Mon. S. Cuore, Testona, Turin, Italy.

Requests for images or relics of Sister Consolata should also be addressed to this convent. Such letters may be written in English.